TELL ME WHY

A Guide to Children's Questions
about Faith and Life

Marilyn Franzen Holm

AUGSBURG Publishing House • Minneapolis

TELL ME WHY
A Guide to Children's Questions about Faith and Life

Library of Congress Cataloging in Publication Data

Holm, Marilyn Franzen, 1944-
  TELL ME WHY.

  Bibliography: p.
  1. Christian education of children.   I. Title.
BV1475.2.H58   1985   248.8'4   85-7355
ISBN 0-8066-2160-5

Manufactured in the U.S.A.   APH 10-6230

1   2   3   4   5   6   7   8   9   0   1   2   3   4   5   6   7   8   9

For my parents,
who tried to answer all my questions
and
my children,
who I hope keep asking them.

CONTENTS

Let It Live

Never kill a question;
it is a fragile thing.
A good question deserves to live.
One doesn't so much answer it as converse with it,
or, better yet, one lives with it.
Great questions are the permanent
and blessed guests of the mind.
But the greatest questions of all
are those which build bridges to the heart,
addressing the whole person.

No answer should be designed to kill the question.
When one is too dogmatic, or too sure,
one shows disrespect for truth
and the question which points toward it.
Beyond my answer there is always more,
more light waiting to break in,
and waves of inexhaustible meaning
ready to break against wisdom's widening shore.
Wherever there is a question, let it live!

From *Bless My Growing* by Gerhard Frost, copyright © 1974 Augsburg Publishing House

PREFACE

It seemed very simple before I had children. The mistakes and inconsistencies of parents appeared so avoidable. Then I had children of my own and became a foster mother to many more. Gradually, one of the best-kept secrets around was revealed to me—just how difficult it really is to be a parent—a *good* parent.

A German proverb says, "It is easy to *become* a parent, but difficult to *be* one." We think we're somehow born with necessary knowledge. Good parenting, it seems, should be as natural as breathing. But then, when the going gets rough, we become frustrated and feel awful. Instead of having all the answers, we have mostly questions: "Why can't I be a better parent?" "Why doesn't my child act like I think she should?" "How can I prepare my son for the future?"

Few people are willing to admit what a tough job parenting can be, especially when they think everyone else is doing a better job. It's easy to become discouraged and frightened when society is changing around us at a breakneck rate.

The purpose of this book is to encourage you, to help you use "the teachable moments" of your child's questions. The truth is, parents teach in the toughest but most rewarding school in the world, the "school for making people" (Virginia Satir). When we realize that childhood is the time foundations for life are laid—for bad or for good—that responsibility can be overwhelming.

And when our children come at us with questions: "If I wasn't me, who would I be?" "What will we do all the time in heaven?" "Why did the Jensen's baby die?" then we really know our limitations. What do we teach our children about faith, about the world? What is really important to teach our children? How do we give them both *roots* and *wings—roots* that help them build their lives on solid values, *wings* that permit independence and maturity in an age when technology challenges basic attitudes and beliefs? With the changes that such technology brings, we seek what is important and eternal for our children.

This book will help you understand a few simple principles of reaching and teaching children. It will suggest ways you can welcome your child's questions not as annoyances, but as "teachable moments" when you share your trust in God's love and purposes for all people.

INTRODUCTION

A mother and two sons had come to my office to talk about placing the older boy in foster care. Described by his mother as "a hopeless case," he sat staring at the floor, refusing to talk about the hurt and anger he felt toward his mother. The younger boy, an energetic preschooler, provided a dramatic contrast to his brother. "What does that say?" he'd ask, pointing to a poster on my wall. "Who's that?" he said as a secretary walked by. "What are all those books about?" he wondered as he examined the bookshelves. The questions addressed to the mother went ignored by her as I tried talking with the older brother. Finally, in exasperation, she screamed at the preschooler, "Shut up! Can't you see I don't want to talk to you!"

The interaction with the small boy saddened me nearly as much as the anger and alienation existing between the older boy and his mother. It seems safe to say that based on the attitudes revealed to her younger son, in a few years we will have a similar situation in this office with the two of them. Though she might dearly love her children, neither one experienced or felt that love. The way she ignored, then shouted at, her younger child clearly showed her to be unwilling or unable to use his questions as a way of building relationships, of teaching him.

This book attempts to equip you so that you can deal with children's questions about faith and life. In doing this you will be giving a child an unshakable foundation in a time of unprecedented change.

Why in the world do we need another book about children? Countless new titles are issued every year that tell us how to be a better parent, how to discipline or not discipline, how to help children get along with others. The list goes on endlessly. After reading dozens of such books, I feel inadequate and ineffective. And from my experiences as a mother, foster mother, and family social worker, many of these books seem totally unrealistic. The situations many of them deal with never existed in our home and probably don't in yours, either.

On the other hand, if your home is anything like ours, you have children who ask questions from the time they are able to form words. These questions continue as the children grow older, and they never get easier. But when a child asks you, "If God can do anything, why doesn't he help me get better grades?" or "How do I know if I'm a Christian?" or "Why did God make me?" that small person is open in a special, unique way to what you have to say. It's that "teachable moment" when you have an opportunity, such as at no other time, to share with the child your love, God's love, and values and attitudes for which we live and die.

The great thing about using your child's questions for nurture and faith development is that you don't need to own a computer or data bank or even a college degree. All you need is love and honesty and a child who asks questions. After all, every normal child is born curious. Already in the hospital nursery children manipulate and explore their new environment. Using their mouths at first, and then, with increasing sophistication, their other senses, newborns attempt to make sense of their world. A child who comes home to parents who welcome and reward curiosity is off to a good start in life.

What does your child want to know? In a word, everything. This book does not set out to give every possible answer to every conceivable question your child might ask. That would be a task such as the Gospel writer describes: "If they were all written down one by one, I suppose that the whole world could not hold the books that would be written" (John 21:25 TEV). Instead, this book will encourage you to participate in your child's learning through appreciating, respecting, loving, challenging, and listening.

A few general comments

Most young children's questions are about the names of things and places. Each new name is a valuable addition to the child's collection of words, and he or she will use it over and over, often to the point of nearly driving parents to distraction.

Keep in mind that preschool children are unable to understand figures of speech and figurative language. The writings of child psychologists such as Piaget suggest that preschoolers learn in personal, concrete ways. Imagine the distress of a small boy who was told he had his father's eyes. In this boy's literal mind, his father must be sightless if the son "had his eyes." When you answer preschooler's questions, then, take care to speak in concrete terms easily understood. If your four-year-old hears you speak of "losing your temper," the child might well start searching for it.

The questions of very young children often involve manipulation of language rather than requests for information. They come from a child's need for competence, a concept discussed in Chapter 2. By age three or four, the average child is a walking question box: "Why is the sky blue?" "Where do the stars go in the daytime?" By five or six, most children have formed their basic attitudes not only toward learning, but toward life in general. It's easy to see, then, that the parents' reaction to early questioning and exploration helps determine the quality of that child's later life.

By age five or six, children have pretty much unconsciously decided that life is either a wondrous, exciting adventure, something they are capable of entering into, or something that is scary and hostile, to be avoided as much as possible. Questions may be asked, then answered, by a child of six, based on perceptions of the world at that point.

A youngster preoccupied with the mountainous landscape around his home was watching his mother one day as she worked with scraps of material left over from garments she'd made earlier. Carefully she pieced together enough for doll clothes for the boy's sister. "Is that where the hills came from, mom?" he asked. "Did the hills come from leftover mountains?" The answer he provided for himself showed how he fit larger questions into the smaller world of which he'd learned at home.

Although many questions asked by primary-age children are intended to gain information, they may have other purposes. When your six-year-old daughter asks, "What would happen to me if you died?" she wants you to put her fears and insecurities to rest as much or more as she wants factual information. When your five-year-old son asks, "Do you love dad more than me?" he is asking for attention, for reassurance. A time such as this provides the "teachable moment" to talk about kinds of love, including the love of God which makes us his children (1 John 3:1).

Until children reach preadolescence, they continue to think that their parents have all the answers. In very young children's minds, this parental ability verges on being godlike. The story has been told of a young child and his mother preparing to call the grandmother in a faraway city. As the mother dialed the number, the child asked her excitedly, "What is grandma doing right now?" The mother laughingly told the child she had no idea. "But why *don't* you know?" the child continued, offended by the gap in mother's omniscience.

More about the teachable moment

You've been thinking about your need for a raise, finally deciding to ask the following morning. You arrive at the office to find the boss in a terrible temper, furious over losing an important contract, one in which you were involved. Would you go ahead and ask for that raise right then? Probably not. Or your spouse calls you just to say, "I love you." Would you choose that moment to air some old grievance? I hope not! Most of us sense how important the timing is on such occasions. Yet too often we parents show an amazing lack of sensitivity to our children, demanding, scolding, or nagging them at the worst possible times.

For example, my son Erik comes home from football practice exhilarated over the praise given him by his coach. I nod at him, not really listening, scarcely able to wait to begin the lecture I've been rehearsing since discovering the wet towels dropped on the bathroom floor. Does this sound unhappily familiar? Maybe you, too, have been guilty of deciding for children the times when they are ready to learn, instead of waiting for the teachable moment.

The Greek language has two words for time: *chronos* and *kairos*. *Chronos* shows up in our language in such words as *chronicle* and *chronic;* it is a measurement or quantity word. *Kairos,* on the other hand, implies not quantity but quality, appropriateness, or ripeness, as implied in the expression, "Make hay while the sun shines." The best teaching occurs when parents are alert for the *kairos* or teachable moment for learning. This is the time when everything is right for affection or correction, guidance or challenge. How can you recognize this teachable moment? You learn it with practice. You can learn to tune in to the curiosity and mood of your child, to hear what is really being asked.

Unfortunately, I see in my own and other families a tendency to praise at a time when kids least need praise, to instruct when they aren't interested, and to correct at the times they already feel bad about themselves. The time to point out the mistakes on a composition is not when the child comes home upset over a poor grade. That's the time for affirmation and praise. Instead of finding errors, you might offer comfort: "I can tell you care a lot about doing well in English. I'm happy that you want to do well. I'll help you with your paper later. How about having a snack with me now and telling me about the rest of your day?"

I noticed a beautiful example of a mother using the teachable moment with her child not long ago in a shopping mall. A mother and daughter of perhaps eight were sitting, apparently waiting for someone, when another mother and her young son came walking in their direction. The boy appeared to be having a very difficult time maneuvering on crutches and braces, his spastic and uncontrolled movements often working against his purposes. The mother calmly helped him several times, but mostly seemed to be speaking encouragingly as they made their laborious way. The little girl watching this scene was appalled. After a time I heard her ask her mother, "If that boy's mother really loved him, wouldn't she carry him?"

Her mother smiled at her. "I know it looks as though she might be unkind to him. Can you think, though, why it's important that he learn to walk for himself?" Before long, the child had come up with reasons with which the boy's mother probably would have agreed. The teachable moment had been well used. This could also have been a perfect opportunity to draw a comparison with God's apparent lack of intervention in our lives at the instant we request it. The boy with the disability seemed to trust his mother and to look to her for encouragement, not to carry him through the mall. Do we as parents share with our children that same trusting attitude toward God?

Some suggestions for answering questions

1. Don't overwhelm your child with information. Be sensitive to just how much is really requested (if indeed, the question is for facts).

A father who was by occupation a newscaster was asked by his small son how he got into the TV every night. The father went into a lengthy technical explanation of how television works, assuring the boy he never crawled into the set. When at last the father had finished, the son eyed him with an even more puzzled look. "But dad, how do you get *out*, then?" The boy hadn't heard a word of the father's inappropriate answer. The old story about the child who asks about penguins, ending with the lament, "But I didn't want to know *that* much about penguins!" should be one we keep in mind when we answer children's questions.

2. Keep your answers consistent with the mental development of the child. Many good books can help you understand your child's level of development. It is useless, for example, to use logical argument and evidence to answer a four-year-old's question. The child's mind depends on what can be seen or heard or touched.

3. Remember that children hear our words in a fresh and original way, so keep your sense of humor handy! My husband and five-year-old John were walking through a horse pasture at grandma's farm in Wisconsin when John stepped into something and shuddered.

"What's that?" he pointed.

"Horse apples," his dad answered, still walking.

"Horse apples? What's that?" John persisted.

"Horse manure," dad tried again. John was quiet for a few seconds, thinking this over.

"Horsemen who're—*what*?" came his puzzled reply. He had heard an answer quite different from that his father thought he was giving.

4. Don't be afraid to admit you don't know. Kids' questions reflect both the triumphs and tragedies of childhood, and they deserve a two-way conversation more than a one-word answer. "I don't know for sure. What do you think?" might be the best answer for some questions.

5. Do more listening and less talking. In his book *If I Were Starting My Family Again,* John M. Drescher reports that the average child asks 500,000 questions by the age of 15. "What a privilege for parents—a half million opportunities to share something about the meaning of life."

He goes on to explain how important listening is for parents, listening with what he refers to as the "third ear." "I'd seek to hear what my child was feeling if he asked questions or made statements." We as parents need to be sensitive to those questions left unspoken, those feelings left unexpressed.

As we listen, it's important that the child *knows* we are listening. The best way to do that is through eye contact. Nodding and mumbling while still reading the newspaper, peeling potatoes, or watching television does not communicate listening. I can remember when our daughter Katie was small, and one afternoon her interminable questions eventually met with several unthinking answers on my part. After a time, she came over to where I was sitting and turned my face with her little hands to look at her. "I'm talking, mom, but you're not hearing," she told me. It was true.

6. While the child should be aware that we as parents are willing to help, something else is very important. It is best for both if the child is allowed to learn for himself or herself whenever possible. We cannot always be around to answer questions, no matter how attentive and loving we be. That's why

more important than knowing facts is the child's growing ability to perceive, to draw conclusions, to grow in faith.

Finally, Charlie Shedd's words from *Promises to Peter* provide a point of view for parents to use as they answer their children's questions:

> I promise you that I will never say no if I can possibly say yes,
> I pledge that I will really be with you when I am with you,
> I pledge also that I will try to see things from a child's point of view.

1

SOME QUESTIONS FOR PARENTS

Most parents are aware that we teach our children every day, whether or not we intend to. By the way we spend our time we teach them what is important to us. We teach them by what we do and don't talk about. We teach them that our faith is central to our lives, or that it isn't worth sharing with them.

Some parents do want to share their faith and encourage its development with their children, but don't feel comfortable in doing so for a number of reasons. They find talking with children about God embarrassing or artificial.

Another obstacle is the chaotic, fragmented quality of family life today. Some families, my own included, can sometimes go for more than a day without having everyone together at the same time other than for sleeping. When Katie gets home from Children's Chorale, Erik's at football practice. By the time he gets home, I've left to lead a weekly support group for adolescent incest victims. When I get home, dad will have departed for a church building committee meeting. It takes teeth-gritting discipline and organization to keep a special family time these days. When these all-together family times are infrequent, as they are for most families today, it is even more important that short interactions with individual children be meaningful. God can be shared, after all, in everyday words and spontaneous situations.

However, before we can share our faith with a child, we need to ask ourselves some questions, perhaps questions we haven't thought much about. In his excellent book, titled with a question that should touch the heart of every parent, *Will Our Children Have Faith?*, John Westerhoff states, "The most important questions a person can ask are: How can I be what I say I am? How can I live what I profess? There ought to be some identifiable difference between the person who claims the name of Christ and someone who denies him. If we are truly in Christ, there should be qualities, characteristics, dispositions, and understanding discernible in our inner and outer lives."

This brings us to some other questions for parents: If I am truly in Christ, what do I teach my child about God, about himself? What do I teach her about other people, about the world?

After thinking a bit, I come up with the following list of what I'd like to teach my own children. I'd like to lead them to experience:

- faith as central to life, love of God made concrete in loving and serving others;
- a feeling of being loved and competent;
- satisfying, caring relationships with several people;
- balance between individual (self-reliance) and community (interdependence);
- enjoyment and meaning both in life work and leisure;
- ability to adapt while retaining unchanging values.

This list isn't necessarily the one I would have made a year ago or might compose next year. You might try making your own list, then see how your priorities change in a year. We need to be aware of what is important to ourselves as parents if we are to put our beliefs into everyday situations a child can grasp.

Ideally, children will hear and see their parents modeling what they wish to teach. Parents will, for example, bring faith into everyday occurrences, demonstrate kindness, recognize their own uniqueness and that of the child, and show a zest for living in God's creation.

It may be surprising to some that the condition of growing up in a home where God is spoken of frequently will not in and of itself produce healthy, happy, well-adjusted children. If the God spoken of is one who is more like a bogeyman ready to pounce on innocent victims than a merciful, forgiving father, the child may grow up fearful and neurotic.

Jack was 10 when he came to live with us. He had gone through life to that point as a "disposable child," one parent or stepparent after another throwing him on someone else's doorstep. He eventually was sent to a residential "Christian school," advertising itself as "strong on discipline." He heard plenty about God at that school. That was also the place he tried to commit suicide, which was enough to scare the school officials into sending him back to his home county, the point at which we got to know him.

Jack's tale was one of casual brutality in the name of Christianity. He had gone for 36 hours without food at the school because he had not memorized the required number of Bible verses. He had gone through the "water treatment," a punishment he refused to talk about. The constant barrage of hellfire and brimstone left this boy understandably reluctant to come live in the home of a pastor and his family. However, severely depressed and considered by psychiatrists to be at high risk for suicide without intervention, he didn't have many choices. While he lived with us for assessment of his situation, we tried to help him see himself as lovable, as competent, as worthwhile. These ideas were new to him, and God worked a miracle in this boy. Now he's moved to a long-term placement and will probably eventually be adopted by those loving parents who have helped him learn of a God who loves and cares. He's a perfect example of how plenty of "religious talk" doesn't necessarily produce a healthy, happy child who grows in grace and love to God. Indeed, the cruel, punitive God he heard about nearly cost him his life.

As part of our investigative procedure at the social-services agency where I work, dolls are used for children to play with when sexual abuse is suspected. Children who have been physically or sexually abused will often reveal more through these dolls than through direct questioning by social workers. One boy playing with these dolls while his mother talked to another worker caught my eye as he set them up in a line leaning along the wall. When they were adjusted to his satisfaction, he leaned down toward them and imitating his mother's voice, warned them. "Now, you say your prayers, do you hear? And you tell God everything you did wrong. If you don't, you can die and go to hell."

The mother looked over at her child approvingly. This was obviously the view of God she was teaching her child, a God who would capriciously destroy a child who forgot to mention a transgression. She was teaching her child a view of God at odds with what the Bible reveals to me.

What is your view of God? Ask yourself just what you believe about God and how this translates into how you see yourself. Because of what God has done for you and me in sending his Son to die for us, I believe people are intrinsically lovable and valuable. They have worth in God's eyes, and therefore we have worth in each other's eyes. Furthermore, since God gives us gifts and abilities, we are expected to use them wisely and well. What we do should make a difference in our lives and the lives of others.

What do you believe about the lovability and worth of people, of your child? Is it unconditional, or is it dependent on some quality or performance?

And what about the lives of our children, their futures in the 21st century? Lasers and atoms are being put to both beneficial and destructive uses never dreamed of a few years ago. New methods of education using computers and electronic marvels will revolutionize their schools. The questions for parents in this area are: What do we want our children to learn? How can we educate children for a world that will change so rapidly as to defy our comprehension? What of the past is worth preserving? What qualities, values, and skills should be transmitted? Such questions are far too important to leave to professional educators. They must be answered by parents and taught to children spontaneously, frequently, comfortably, in the home.

2

DO YOU LOVE ME WHEN I'M BAD?

Comments on Self-Esteem and Discipline

It was one of those social gatherings where the men huddle around the TV football game while the women cluster in another room to talk. Before long the women's conversation shifted to the shooting in another town of a father by a son and daughter whom for years he'd allegedly abused.

"What a tragedy," one woman said. "The father is dead, both children facing sentences for killing him. And you wonder how many years of misery went on before this happened."

The faces in the group grew sober. Then came one woman's wistful voice: "Wouldn't it be wonderful if there was some magic formula to make sure kids grow up feeling good about themselves? There would be no child abuse."

Although her words were spoken wishfully, in fact such a formula does exist. Social scientists are overwhelmingly coming to the conclusion that productive, well-adjusted people possess one factor in common: a high degree of self-esteem.

Social class, financial status, intelligence, race, or geography have nothing to do with a person's self-esteem. It is almost entirely present or absent in a child because of what the parents see in that child—or more importantly, what the child *thinks* they see.

If you are like most parents, you wish more for your child than mere avoidance of delinquent behavior stemming from abuse, alcoholism, or promiscuity. You hope your child will be happy, get along well with people, and someday be ready to face responsibly the world without you. You're probably aware of many dreams and expectations you hold for your child. What you're maybe *not* certain about is how to help your child attain these hopes and dreams. Fortunately, the key to such attainment is there for any parent who wants it.

The evidence is clear. The basic difference between a person who flounders through life, existing from crisis to crisis, and a person who lives a competent, meaningful life is the internal picture of individual worth carried by each person. It is necessary not only for your child's individual development, but for satisfying relationships throughout his or her life. When children experience high self-esteem, they do well, feel and look good, and respond to everyone around them in positive ways.

What is self-esteem?

One of the best definitions I've run across explains self-esteem as how you feel about yourself *privately*. When you look in the mirror, do you like who you see? If so, you probably have a high degree of self-esteem. High self-esteem is not an egotistical, overblown sense of one's own importance. It is not boastful conceit. A conceited person may appear to others to have a high sense of self-esteem. Actually, if it exists, it shows itself in a quiet sense of value and self-respect. People who are considered conceited or braggarts are only desperately buttressing their own dislike of self by trying to convince others of their worth.

Stanley Coopersmith, a professor of psychology known for

his prodigious work in the area of self-esteem, describes this behavior as caused by a "soft, weak center of uncertainty which is surrounded by a tougher, masking outer layer—a disguise."

Self-esteem is not self-centeredness, condescension, machismo, or showing off. All these are a whitewash to cover low self-esteem. People who have high self-esteem know they are *lovable* and *capable,* as will be explained. They care about themselves. Because they feel good about themselves, they can care about others. They do not build themselves up at the expense of others—exploiting, gossiping, patronizing. They unconsciously organize their lives around the message, "I am worthwhile." They trust themselves and others and face life positively.

Compassion, self-control, servanthood, responsibility—all flow easily from persons who have high self-esteem. Persons who feel they matter, that the world is a better place because they are here, can reach out to others. To such persons, life makes sense, and they possess a degree of control over what will happen. Those people have a resiliency and faith in their own competence that make them ready for anything life can bring. A person with high self-esteem can say with Paul, "I have learned to be content whatever the circumstances" (Phil. 4:11).

Some Christians may have trouble with the idea of self-esteem being desirable. After all, we sing about "amazing grace that saved a wretch like me." How can we reconcile this with "I am worthwhile"? The history of the church is replete with examples of how Christians have overemphasized the inherent sinfulness of humanity. Psalm 8 reminds us that sinful though we be, desperately in need of God's grace, we have an inestimable value. "You made him [humanity] a little lower than the heavenly beings and crowned him with glory and honor" (Ps. 8:5). To emphasize our wretchedness to the exclusion of verses such as these denigrates the very jewel of God's creation, humanity.

The concept of self-esteem explains much of people's behavior and is based on a simple premise: most of what a person does is motivated by the desire to feel good about himself or herself. That desire to feel good will influence the kind of friends the person chooses, the way he or she acts in school and on the job, the kind of person he or she marries. A person's high self-esteem or lack of it will directly influence all aspects of his or her life. Most authorities on child development today agree that self-esteem is the crucial factor that determines a child's failure or success in life.

How do we get high self-esteem?

Because the family is the primary place where we decide who we are and what we're like, the parenting we received or bestow is important. The messages we send our children from infancy largely determine their self-esteem. How do we make sure we're building self-esteem in our child?

High self-esteem comes from two convictions: *I am lovable* and *I am capable*. Both are necessary for the child to truly feel worthy.

The first concept seems obvious. Given the number of articles and books available in the last years, few parents today can be unaware of the importance of loving nurture for their infant. Even among the severely neglectful mothers with whom I work, few would admit to not loving their children. Yet the mere fact that a child is loved by parents is not necessarily enough to develop high self-esteem. The child must *feel* loved, and, even with conscientious parents, that is not always the case.

Parents who have sacrificed for their child, who have spent endless nights rocking that colicky baby, who have endlessly tutored in math, and who have repeatedly said, "I love you," are sometimes dazed to find that the child doesn't feel loved.

Despite having parents who deeply care, the child may not *feel* genuinely loved.

What gets in the way of feeling loved? According to Dr. Ross Campbell, author of *How to Really Love Your Child,* many children of Christian parents are well-disciplined but feel unloved. He explains that these parents have confused discipline with punishment, and as a result these well-meaning people have not conveyed their love to their children. While they may have taken seriously the need to punish misbehavior when it occurs, they have often done so at the expense of making the child feel loved conditionally. The truth is, most of children's misbehavior stems from a sense of not having enough positive attention (love).

I can sense the defensive reaction from many readers: "What? Is she saying a kid won't misbehave if he's loved, that it's *my* fault Johnny's so naughty?" Well, yes and no. Sometimes. Certainly we are born sinful creatures, born of a fallen humanity. But within that framework, inappropriate love from parents can lead to low self-esteem and consequently, unacceptable behavior.

Some people maintain it's impossible to give a child too much love. Others say too much love can spoil a child. Who's right?

Too much *inappropriate* love can certainly "spoil" a child. It does not meet a child's basic emotional needs, and problems are sure to follow. In my job as family social worker, I'm exposed often to extreme examples of how inappropriate love can not only cripple the child but even lead to the breakdown of the family. As a mother, I try to be aware if the love I feel for my children begins to be expressed inappropriately.

We can identify six types of inappropriate love that often overlap.

1. *Possessive love.* Probably a parent doesn't exist who hasn't referred to "my baby" or "our child." Yet we need to remember that we don't *own* our children, that we have an

obligation to prepare children to live their own lives, to develop judgment, to be independent of us.

What happens if a parent consistently sees his child as property? The child may grow up unable to make decisions, or crave authoritarianism into adulthood. Such a person is ripe for cult involvement or membership in any fanatical group that tells him or her what to do and how to do it. Or the young person may rebel, casting away any values that are associated with the parents. Parents who want to really love their child will identify possessive love, try to separate it from their honest caring, and do what they can to help the child become self-reliant.

2. *Seductive love.*   At the time I write this, I'm involved in leading two support groups for teenage incest victims. These girls, who represent only a small percentage of those appropriate for such groups, almost all share the situation of having been seduced by fathers or other trusted family members. With few exceptions did the incest which now disturbs them begin in the reprehensible way it ended. Almost uniformly the incest began with inappropriate touching or caressing on the part of these men. Gradually, the situation became more and more overtly sexual, with increasing emotional cost inflicted on the young victims.

Because many of these girls now live in foster homes, their foster fathers are often terrified of getting anywhere near them for fear their actions might be misunderstood. Yet these children desperately need appropriate touching, just as do your own children, to reassure them of their worth.

Parents who are generous with hugs and kisses have children with much higher self-esteem than the average, a recent PTA study found. Bumper stickers asking if you've hugged your child today remind parents commuting to work or shopping to take the time to touch the people we care most about.

The solution to inappropriate, seductive love is not avoidance of all physical contact. Being touched and held never stops being the primary expression of love among humans. To truly feel loved, children especially need appropriate, frequent, non-prolonged touch.

3. *Vicarious love.*   Sometimes parents wish for their child to do the things they couldn't do, to have the opportunities that eluded them. The definition of vicariousness explains the problem: it means finding meaning for one's life through the life of another. And for the child who feels he has the responsibility of living his life so as to satisfy his parent, the cost can be frightfully high.

Kim, one of the girls with whom I work, is a victim of her mother's vicarious love. This mother, who evidently never experienced admiration, respect, or love from men, had unconsciously decided early in her daughter's life that things would be different this time. Kim's mother vicariously relived her own loveless adolescence but this time through Kim who became involved in one relationship after another with young men. Kim soon came to realize that her worth was measured by the number of boys who came around, the value of gifts they brought, and their professions of love. To earn her mother's love, Kim constantly found herself in circumstances she wasn't able to handle. When she came home one day in tears announcing her pregnancy, Kim's mother marched her off for an abortion and warned her to be more careful after this. As Dr. Campbell writes, "We must love our child so he can fulfill God's plan for his life, not our vicarious one."

4. *Role-reversed love.*   One of the most challenging parts of my occupation is instead of going to court to fight out a termination of parental rights, to convince the parents that voluntary relinquishment of parental rights is the best, most loving act they can do for that child. This is what I tried to do in the case of a mother and daughter who had a role-reversed love.

Peggy is the third child of a mother who's had many marriages and currently lives in a faraway city with her boyfriend.

The mother and Sam left town nearly a year ago, putting 12-year-old Peggy in the care of her 18-year-old sister. Shortly before that, Peggy had begun complaining to family members about Sam's sexual advances, and rather than face an investigation, her mother and Sam left the state. After a few weeks the older sister felt she could no longer handle the responsibility of Peggy and reported the situation to social services.

When I finally obtained an address and wrote the mother asking her to consider relinquishing Peggy so she might be adopted by the loving family then caring for her, the mother responded in a fury. "I had to leave with Sam," she explained. "Do you think Peggy will take care of me when I'm old? I need to take care of myself. She won't!"

This situation is fairly typical of a role-reversed love. The mother loved her daughter only so long as the daughter didn't interfere with her own needs. Instead of Peggy finding nurture and security from her parent, this mother expected her to meet *her* needs, to keep the family together through compliant silence. Again, this abandonment might seem an extreme example of what can happen in role-reversed love. More frequently, we find parents who occasionally expect their children to make them feel good, especially at the time of stress or unhappiness such as divorce or death. When we are overworked or discouraged, it's easy to become so drained that instead of being parents to our children, we expect them to comfort and support us emotionally. When we want our children to meet our emotional needs, we are on dangerous ground. If we recognize this as happening, we'd better look to our spouse or adult friends to give us the love we're unfairly trying to get from our child.

5. *Earned love.*   Does a parent exist who doesn't love a child—but with occasional strings attached? "If only you'd . . ." "I wish you would . . . " messages, spoken or not, are perceived by the child as conditional love. "I'll love you if you

behave," is a message every child has heard at one time or another. Consequently, the child sees his or her worth as based on behavior or performance, rather than on self. And whenever personal worth depends on performance, personal value is questioned with every misdeed or failure to meet a standard.

Every day, in dozens of ways, the child asks, "Do you love me?" Rarely is it asked verbally; instead, it is asked through the child's behavior. If we love the child unconditionally (though not always his or her behavior), the child knows the answer: "Yes, I love you, no matter what." If the child hears an answer that says, "I love you if . . . " or "I love you when. . . ," the child is not reassured of his or her worth. The child is uncertain and will keep asking that question, often with more unsettling acts, which create more conditional answers. A vicious cycle has been set in motion.

How can parents convey unconditional love? The answer is, we can't always. We are ourselves selfish, sinful creatures who at times, let's face it, care more about our own feelings. But if we are truly committed to the ideal of loving our child unconditionally, we can approach the goal. We can love the child while at the same time teaching limits and discipline. The two are not mutually exclusive!

Dr. Campbell writes that if we love our children only when they please us (conditional love) and convey that love to them only during those times, they will not feel genuinely loved. This creates insecurity, damages their self-esteem, and actually prevents them from moving onto better self-control and more mature behavior. Therefore, their behavior and its development is not only their responsibility, but the parent's as well.

In answer to the question, "Is it my fault that Johnny's so naughty?" we can see that part of the problem may lie with the parents. If parents are usually able to convey unconditional love, chances are Johnny will generally feel good about himself and learn to behave in an age-appropriate way.

6. *Noncherishing love.*   I was rather absently dusting the living room furniture the other day when the neighbors across the street caught my attention. The young father was tossing his toddler in the air, and the mutual enjoyment they were experiencing was a pleasure to watch. The joy the father expressed—as seen in his smiles, laughter, hugs, and eye contact—could be described as *cherishing*.

Thinking how rarely one sees this type of parent-child interaction made me sad. Most of parental love for children seems directed at correcting, changing, or physically caring for them. How little do most of us cherish our children in a way that lets them know how dearly they are loved, cherish them in such a way they know just how special and irreplaceable they are to us.

Most parents do feel their children are unique and loved. If our children were to be snatched away by death or kidnapping, we would be devastated and realize just how much we do love them. Yet, many children feel noncherished, some barely tolerated, by the way we treat them. How many of us would have any friends if we treated them the way we treat our children? We often shame, nag, ignore, or belittle them in a way we wouldn't dream of doing to even casual acquaintances. Why?

One of the reasons is we just don't think about children as having feelings. We ignore the fact, as Dr. Seuss puts it, that "after all, a person's a person, no matter how small." Most parents forget to put themselves in their children's shoes and think about how they'd feel if they were treated the way they treat their children—often with disrespect, sometimes with scorn.

A second reason our children don't feel cherished is because we concentrate on what our children aren't or don't have, rather than on their uniqueness, what they are and can do. I cringe inside thinking of the rat-a-tat of my morning's criticism: "Don't make so much noise when you eat." "How many times have I told you to put your dishes in the dishwasher?" "Why can't you be more pleasant in the morning?" (That one should have been directed back at myself!)

Why don't I concentrate on the positive? "I'm glad you got up without my having to call you." "Thanks for putting away the cereal and milk." "You look especially nice this morning." When was the last time I said out loud, "I'm happy to be with you," "I'm glad you're part of our family," "You make me feel special"? So often the thoughts that fill my heart don't make it to my lips.

One way we can help our children feel cherished is to give recognition for what they are and can do and refuse to focus on what they are not or what they can't do. As you will see, this does *not* mean we don't give guidance or correction.

A third reason we don't cherish our children is that we don't see their good qualities. The children who most urgently need cherishing are usually those least likely to be well-behaved and act lovably. If you feel at wit's end with your child, unable to see much worth cherishing, imagine that child as belonging to a friend or neighbor. Sometimes it's easier to see lovable qualities from this perspective.

If we can make our children feel cherished by the way we look at them, speak to them, and prize them, they will have a good start toward the high self-esteem they deserve to experience. They will *feel* loved.

The importance of feeling capable

As described earlier, the child's feeling of being loved and lovable is part of the foundation for high self-esteem. The other requirement is a feeling of competence: "What I do, matters. I can handle what's coming. I'm capable and able to make a difference."

The person who has grown up lacking a sense of competence is easy to spot. He's the one who has erected an impenetrable wall of defensiveness: "It's not my fault! Don't blame me!" She's the woman who is bloblike in her submissiveness: "It was my fault my husband beat me. I burned the roast." Or the person who withdraws into fantasy, never attempting to deal with the real world: "When I win the lottery, everything will be okay." People such as these have grown up lacking a sense of competence. Some characteristics of people who may feel loved but not competent include (1) avoidance of anxiety-producing situations, (2) blame of others for personal failing, (3) put-down of personal abilities, (4) sense of impotence to change anything, and (5) excessive need for others' approval.

The obvious question is, how do we help our children grow up feeling capable? First, if we understand the various stages of child development and the tasks children must learn for each stage, it's easier to know how to help children master appropriate tasks for each age. The infant who reaches for, grasps, then shakes a rattle has accomplished a feat no less important, for example, than the teenager who has earned the money for and purchased a car. Second, we need to encourage children to make or influence decisions about things that are important to them. A child who has never developed judgment by being allowed to choose so much as the day's clothing while living at home will have a difficult time making such decisions as choice of occupation or mate. (On the other hand, requiring children to make crucial decisions beyond their ability to do so will not make them feel competent, but rather set them up for failure.)

The value of enabling children to make appropriate decisions and choices and solve problems cannot be overemphasized. It is the primary way people learn to feel competent. Anyone—child or adult—who has no influence in things important to him or her—is powerless, lacking in self-esteem.

In contrast to many of the parents with whom I work, who are overly permissive, giving their children practically no rules, parents such as myself who have been raised with "the best of care," have a tendency to overprotect and overrestrict children. In the extreme, such parents try to shield their children from every danger—some real, some imagined. They can actually cripple children by denying them the opportunity to test reality. The message the child hears is, "I'm incapable of doing anything for myself. I'm totally dependent on and helpless without mom." (Usually it's mothers who are guilty of this overprotection.) The child never learns to take personal responsibility for consequences of poor choices.

Another way to help children develop a sense of competence is to provide reasonable, clear rules and expectations. If the child understands exactly what is expected or will not be tolerated, he or she will feel more secure and confident. Children without rules live in a scary existence, never knowing where the boundaries lie. Like medieval sailors, they drift through life, wondering when they will sail off the edge of their world.

One of the most subtle and destructive ways of destroying children's self-esteem is to give them their way in everything, especially if they first must beg, plead, and tease for it. Countless times I've seen a child in a supermarket wheedle down the mother who then disgustedly throws the begged-for treat into her cart. The parent's capitulation is usually accompanied by a remark like, "You're a spoiled brat, do you know that?" And, unfortunately, often the people who have contact with that child as the child grows up agree with that assessment.

Overly indulged children grow up to be selfish, inconsiderate, and demanding. If only they whine long enough, they think, they'll get their way. They feel the world exists solely to serve their every wish, and they exploit people for their own ends.

Children such as these have a horrible shock waiting for them, often at the age of five or six, when they finally run into people or institutions unmoved by their demands. They frequently grow into rebellious teenagers, angry at stifling authority. Immediate gratification is their goal.

On the other hand, parents who meet their children's basic emotional, physical, and spiritual needs don't get manipulated by guilt about not providing every new toy or game the child may ask for. They will not be intimidated into acting weak or inconsistent because they wonder deep down if they really love their child.

We can see, then, that a child who grows up feeling loved and competent is basically on track for developing personal control over behavior—the definition of discipline. And punishment, when needed, can be done in a way that doesn't rob the child of self-esteem by stripping him or her of a feeling of love or competence.

Dr. Gerald E. Nelson's book *The One Minute Scolding* is a gem, because it presents a simple, highly effective way to combine appropriate anger and love as a way of teaching children right from wrong. His method leaves both child and parent feeling good about themselves. It tells the child—toddler to teenager—what rule has been broken and how the parent feels about the rule being broken. More importantly, it teaches appropriate behavior in a loving way. It allows the child to learn that feeling anger and expressing it is natural, but these feelings need to be expressed appropriately. The child learns anger need not be held for hours or days. (To maintain anger toward a child for a long time diminishes self-esteem at the very time the child needs it most and is asking, "Do you love me even when I'm bad?")

It seems somewhat surprising to me that many parents still believe corporal punishment is the only effective way to control or shape their children's behavior. Working as I do with abusive families, I often hear angry and baffled parents make remarks such as, "Well, if I can't whip them, how *can* I make them behave?" Part of my job's challenge is to help these parents learn discipline methods that don't jeopardize children's self-esteem. One such method is the use of choices and consequences. It's practical because it can be used for preschool through high-school aged children. It builds, rather than destroys, self-esteem by helping children learn self-control, make sound decisions, change behavior, and develop independent thinking. With choices and consequences, children learn to take responsibility for their own behavior.

I used this choices-and-consequences method recently with Erik, who was choosing to sleep as long as possible every morning, leaving his bed unmade and his room in chaos. He was given the choice of making his bed and picking up his clothes every morning or not doing so. He was told that if he chose not to clean up his room, he would lose the privilege of going to the "Y" Saturday mornings to play basketball. It was his choice. No anger or power struggle was involved. No threat to self-esteem was made.

The most common type of logical or planned consequences involves (1) loss of privilege as above, (2) time-out, and (3) restitution or "making good." Time-outs work best for preschoolers or young children. Having them sit quietly with no entertainment for three to five minutes can be a powerful consequence. Restitution requires children to "make good" for their actions. It is more effective with older children. A child who breaks another's toy because of carelessness may be required to "work off" the cost of buying a new one.

A word of caution: the consequences of behavior must occur each time the behavior occurs. Otherwise, children become confused and don't know what to expect. By consistently using reasonable consequences, parents help children learn healthy ways to control their own behavior.

The following are a few suggestions regarding discipline that have been helpful to me as a mother and foster mother.

1. Be consistent. Do what you say you will. Don't give additional chances. If you say "No TV till the job is finished," don't back down if the room is only half-done.
2. Don't keep resurrecting the crime. Deal with the misbehavior, then bury it.
3. Make expectations clear. Telling the young child to "be home early," for example, leaves room for misunderstanding.
4. The most effective punishment is that which fits the infraction. Make use of logical consequences, for example losing privilege or making restitution.
5. Physical punishment teaches that violence is all right if you are bigger than the victim. It is far less effective than logical consequences.
6. Children who are involved in doing interesting activities are less likely to get into trouble. Parents who know children will be forced to sit for a long period, while waiting at a clinic, for example, should be prepared to provide such activities. A healthy four-year-old cannot sit still staring into space for hours on end. Don't expect behavior of which the child is incapable.
7. Follow punishment with positive reaffirmation of the child's worth and a hug or other physical warmth.

Helping children grow up having high self-esteem and self-discipline requires effort, patience and consistency. Some private prayers and tears don't hurt, either!

A poster in my office says it well: "Kids! You can't beat 'em. Love them. Respect them. Cherish them."

Christianity forms the solid structure on which self-esteem is built. Jesus tells us to love God, and our neighbors as ourselves (Mark 12:29-31). Within the framework of these words, we see ourselves not as better or worse than our neighbors, but equally loved by the Savior who shed his blood for all— young and old, good and bad.

3

WHO WAS GOD'S FATHER?

Questions about God and the Christian Life

Filled with the awesome responsibility of bringing up a child in the faith, Christian parents set out with the best of intentions but often find the task difficult, the right words hard to come by. Religious education, after all, belongs to those trained in theology and education, in an hour a week set aside for that purpose, right? And so, many well-intentioned parents leave faith development to the church school teachers—who may themselves feel unprepared and inadequate.

One wonders how a story that can be told as simply as the good news has become so intimidating, why many of us think we can't talk about God without couching our words in long lectures or difficult theological terms. If this is a problem, we need to remind ourselves that though God's story is so deep and so wide that libraries have been written about it, it is also simple. Children are not looking for or wanting abstract ideas. Jesus reminded his followers that they needed to become like children, which I take to mean that he wanted his truths applied to the everyday, to the practical.

Faith development is an ongoing process, not only for children but for adults. It's a good idea to let our children know that we too still have questions, that our faith is never a finished product, but an experience of searching for the God who wants us to know and love him as much as he knows and loves us.

One of my favorite writers, Frederick Buechner, explains, "Faith . . . is not so much believing this thing or that thing about God as it is hearing a voice that says, 'Come unto me.' We hear the voice, and then we start to go without really knowing what to believe either about the voice or ourselves, and yet we go. Faith is standing in the darkness, and a hand is there, and we take it."

That attitude of trusting in God can best be fostered in the child by parents who have shown themselves trustworthy and accepting of their child and who are aware of their child's needs, especially the spiritual.

In my work with teenagers, I frequently hear a lament about parents, one that keeps me examining my own priorities and how I unconsciously teach religious education to my own children. The lament goes something like this: "My parents make sure I eat the right foods, wear mittens when it's cold, and send me to bed on time, but they don't talk about the most important things, the things I lie awake at night wondering about."

These kinds of statements are not coming from troubled, delinquent adolescents. I hear such words from "good kids," those I teach in church school classes. These teenagers have Christian parents for the most part, ones who evidently feel unable to convey to their children the importance of their own faith. And in today's confused, changing world, children need direction more than ever before. After all, when as parents we have provided everything for a child—food, clothing, love, exercise—we sense a deep-down, searching restlessness that tells us that our basic needs and being are spiritual. St. Augustine's famous words, "Thou hast made us for thyself, O Lord, and our hearts are restless until they find their rest in thee," remind us what is the essential requirement for Christian parents: to share their faith with their children.

A personal relationship with Jesus Christ is the foundation today's children need. It provides meaning and purpose for lives that without it are selfish and empty. Parents cannot overestimate the profound influence on their children of a faith that provides a foundation for their daily living. As parents, we have a unique opportunity to casually, yet powerfully, shape our children's faith. As they ask questions or comment on everyday occurrences, we can reveal how we ourselves love and trust God, look to God for direction as we seek to do his will in the world, and gratefully respond to God's love through service to others.

We should, of course, keep in mind the age and spiritual maturity of the child as we share our faith. One of the best ways to assess a child's spiritual development is to listen to his or her questions, both spoken and unspoken. While your child will probably not expound on theological questions to any length, the underlying concerns will be evident as you listen to everyday conversation and comments.

Below are some questions children often ask and some suggestions as to how you might begin to answer those questions. Your answers, of course, should be consistent with your own beliefs.

Questions about God

How do I know there's a God?

You can never know there's a God in the same way you can know something you see with your eyes or hear with your ears. But through faith, our heart and mind and soul tells us there's a God who is loving and forgiving.

How old is God?

Since God is a spirit, not a person, God wasn't born and doesn't have an age or a birthday. That's hard to understand, because we don't know anything or anyone else that doesn't grow older. God has always been, and will always be.

Where does God live?

God doesn't live in one place. Since God's a spirit God can be everywhere. God lives in you, too. The Bible tells us God's spirit (the Holy Spirit) lives in those who believe in Jesus. Wherever there is love, joy, and peace, God is there.

Who were God's father and mother?

God didn't have a father or mother. One of our creeds says the Father is "uncreated." Nothing existed before him.

Is God married to Mother Nature?

No. God isn't a man, but a spirit. God is real, but Mother Nature is just a way people have of talking about the natural world God created. There is no such person.

Does God really love me?

He certainly does. The Bible says, "See how much the Father has loved us! His love is so great that we are called God's children—and so, in fact, we are" (1 John 3:1 TEV).

Someone said God is really a she. Is that true?

God is neither male nor female, but a spirit. People in the past have usually referred to God as he, but God is not a man.

Does God know my name?

You bet God does. Psalm 139 tells us how well God knows us: "Lord, you have examined me and you know me. You know everything I do; from far away you understand all my thoughts," (vv. 1-2 TEV). God knows what we'll think before we think it! That's how well he knows you.

What is God's telephone number? I'd like to call him.

You don't need a telephone to talk to God. You can talk to God anytime, and unlike your phone that's sometimes busy, God is always ready to listen.

What is the Holy Spirit?

The Holy Spirit is God in you, helping you believe and grow in faith. It is called the Holy Spirit because it is God's spirit.

What's the Holy Ghost, then?

That's another name for the Holy Spirit.

How does God know good people from bad people?

God can see into our hearts and knows we all do bad things at times. God knows who really loves him and tries to please him, because God can see past the outside to what is inside of us, where others can't see.

Why are some people good and others bad?

No person is all good or all bad. Some people seem to be more kind and loving than others. They are allowing God's Spirit to work in them more than the ones you think of as "bad."

Does God like to laugh?

When we look at some of the creatures God made such as the hippopotamus and the platypus, it seems God must have had a sense of humor. And some of the stories in the Bible make us believe that, too!

Is Jesus really God? He was born later.

The Bible is clear that Jesus is really God. John 10:30 tells us that Jesus and the Father are one.

Why does Jesus have so many names?

Jesus is called by many names because he is too wonderful to describe with just one name. He's called Christ, Savior,

Messiah, Lamb of God, the Good Shepherd, to name a few. *Jesus* was his given name, just as Joey or Marcia might be given to a boy or girl today. He is called *Savior* because he saves us from our sin; *Messiah,* because he is God's promised one; *Lamb of God,* because he takes away our sin just as lambs were offered as sacrifices to God for people's sin long ago; *Good Shepherd,* because he loves and cares for his flock (that's us). He's called *Lord* because he is the ruler of our lives. There are many more names you'll learn as you read your Bible.

Does God love people who do terrible things?

Although it makes God sad when anyone does bad things, God loves everyone. Every one of us is a sinner.

Our pastor talks about God's grace a lot. I know he doesn't mean table prayers, but I don't understand what it is.

God's grace means he loves and forgives us freely, no strings attached. God's love and forgiveness is a gift to you and me.

Why did God make mosquitoes and snakes and bugs?

Often people don't like having these creatures around, but they have a purpose in God's creation. For example, insects serve as food for the birds we do enjoy.

Was Jesus really perfect? Didn't he ever do anything wrong, even when he was little?

The Bible tells us that although he was like us in every way, he did not sin. He was tempted though, and knows how hard it is for us to be good on our own. When he was tempted, he prayed to his Father in heaven, setting an example for us.

Could Jesus do magic tricks?

Jesus had power to perform miracles such as healing people who were sick. He didn't use this power just to get attention for himself, though, as a magician in a TV show might. He used his power to help other people.

If Jesus could do anything, why didn't he save himself from dying on the cross?

He certainly could have stopped the crucifixion if he'd tried. But he permitted the soldiers to put him to death because it was part of God's plan. "God loved the world so much that he gave his only Son, so that everyone who believes in him may not die but have eternal life" (John 3:16 TEV).

I don't understand. How does Jesus' dying take away my sin?

God is a God not only of love and mercy but also justice. God could not overlook our sinfulness and selfishness and pretend they weren't there. So he sent his Son, Jesus, to take our sins on himself and die for them. *His* death paid for *our* sins.

If Jesus is with us now, why do people say he is coming again?

Since he rose from the dead and ascended into heaven, he is with us in spirit. At his next coming, he will return in a special way. He will come in glory, and everyone will know then that he is Lord. You can read how it will be in 1 Cor. 15:51-54.

What happened to the people who died before Jesus came? It isn't fair if they can't go to heaven!

Since God loves and cares for everyone, he has power to save those who lived before Jesus came. Hebrews 11 tells us that faith in the Savior to come saved people such as Noah, Abraham, and Moses.

Questions about the Christian life

How can I know if I'm a Christian?

For some people, being a Christian merely means they are not of another religion, for example Hindu. For others, it means they are trying to be a good person. To others, it is someone who goes to church. But the Bible says something else. If you believe in Jesus as Lord, have been baptized, daily ask for forgiveness, and try to live according to God's will, you are certainly a Christian.

How can I know what God wants me to do?

Sometimes it is hard to know, and people have done terrible things saying God told them to do those deeds. A good guideline to follow is found in Micah 6:8: "To act justly and to love mercy and to walk humbly with your God." The more we read God's word and know what he wants for *all* people, the easier it is to know what his will is for the individual Christian.

What do I have to do to be a Christian?

You don't have to *do* anything, anymore than you have to do something to be your parents' son or daughter. But because you love your parents and are grateful for the love they give you, you try to please them. It's the same with God.

What does it mean to be a born-again Christian?

Some Christians believe we are born again when we are baptized, even if we're babies who don't understand what is happening. Others say that only those people who have committed their lives to Christ are born-again Christians.

Mr. Smith doesn't go to church, but he says he's a Christian. Can you never go to church and still be a Christian?

Jesus can look further than our actions, into our hearts. People may have a reason for not going to church. Church attendance doesn't make a person a Christian. At the same time the church is like a family, and people who aren't there are missed. They also miss out themselves.

How do I know if a person who talks about God is telling the truth?

Jesus warned that many false prophets or teachers would try to lead his followers astray. He gave a good suggestion for knowing who they were. He said we would recognize them by their fruits (Matt. 7:16). That means if good things happen, such as love and forgiveness, the person talking about God is probably a good teacher. If good things, or fruits, are produced, the person is probably telling the truth.

What is my conscience? Is it next to my stomach?

Your conscience is the part of you that tells you when you are doing right or wrong. Sometimes your conscience tells you something is wrong and you go ahead and do it anyway. But we usually have a pretty good idea about whether or not we should do something. Your conscience is not a part of your physical body, but part of your spirit.

My parents say they are Christians, but they yell at me and each other sometimes. Can they still be Christians?

Being a Christian does not mean people are perfect. They will continue to sin, but they will not want to sin and are forgiven for their sin. Maybe you have seen the bumper sticker that says, "Christians aren't perfect, they're just forgiven." That's right!

Our pastor said people are the body of Christ. What does that mean?

Just as the body has many parts that work together for the good of the whole body, the church is made up of many people who work and love each other. All people are important in the church, just as everything in your body from your little toe to your brain is important for your body to work at its best.

Once in Sunday school our teacher told us we were saints. I thought a saint was someone who was very good and then died.

Christians alive or dead can be called saints. It just means their sins are forgiven and they are believers. You can see how the word was used in Bible times by reading Paul's greeting to the Corinthians (1 Cor. 1:1-2).

One of my friends told me his brother didn't want to be a Christian because then he couldn't have any fun.

This is an idea many non-Christians have. They think being a Christian means things you can't do. That attitude must make Jesus very sad. He says that he came that we might have life and have it more abundantly or richly (John 10:10).

Which commandment is most important? You shall not kill?

Jesus said he was giving a new commandment that summed up all the others. He said we should love him above all things, and our neighbor as ourselves. Then he went on to explain our neighbor is anyone who is in need, not just the people who live next door.

I don't like my neighbor at all. She's mean and crabby. How can I love her?

Jesus made it clear we don't have to like everything some people do, especially if it's wrong. At the same time, we can care about that person, be helpful and friendly and forgiving. That's what real loving is.

If God is everywhere, why do we worship him in a church?

We can and should worship God anywhere, but when we gather in a special place with other Christians, we experience the togetherness of "the body of Christ."

Someone told me the church is not a building but people. Is that right?

We sometimes refer to the building where we meet as believers as "the church." But the church is much more than that. It's all the people on earth who love God and share that love, faith, and hope in the future with other believers.

I heard a man say he couldn't go to church because he didn't have good enough clothes. Does God care what we wear to church?

God looks deeper than what we are wearing. No one should

stay home from church or make other people feel less than welcome because of clothing. Jesus would never have done that.

Why do I have to be quiet in church?

There are times to be quiet so others can pray and listen to God's Word. There are times during the singing that you should sing out with enthusiasm!

Why are there so many kinds of churches?

Many time believers have disagreed about the way the Bible should be understood or how God should be worshiped, or many other such things. Eventually different denominations (types of churches) have begun because of such disagreements.

Is there one church that's right? Is it our church?

Our Lord does not have many churches, he has one church. It is made up of many denominations such as Methodist, Baptist, and Lutheran; each tries to be faithful to God and the Bible. Some denominations seem to be closer to what Jesus wanted for his church than others, but probably no one denomination has been completely and always right.

Why was I baptized?

For many reasons. Jesus told us to baptize people in the name of the Father, Son, and Holy Spirit. It washes away our sins and makes us clean in the sight of God. It also makes us members of the body of Christ.

Why do we say the Lord's Prayer and the Creed as a group?

It's a way of expressing that we as believers pray for and believe in the same things. We're united as the body of Christ when we pray and say the Creed together.

Does the pastor work only on Sunday mornings?

Pastors work all week doing such things as planning for

classes and sermons, visiting the sick, meeting with people who help with the work of the congregation, and many other things to serve God and help people.

Does the pastor get all the money in the collection plate?
The pastor gets a salary that's decided on by church members. Most of the money given in church goes for things such as paying building expenses, feeding hungry people, paying for church and Sunday school supplies, and so on.

What is the church year?
The church year is different from the calendar year. It begins with Advent, four Sundays before Christmas, when we begin to prepare for the birth of Jesus. It is followed by the seasons of Christmas, Epiphany, Lent, Easter, and Pentecost.

Why is Easter on a different date each year?
Many hundreds of years ago when the church was new, its leaders decided that Easter would be celebrated on the first Sunday after the first full moon in the spring. Since the dates of full moons change, that changes the date we celebrate.

What is Lent?
It's the 40 weekdays before Easter when we especially think about how Jesus suffered and died for us and what that means for our lives.

My friend gives up something for Lent. Should I do that?
This idea is an old one in the church. It can be very good, but we need to remember that what we do or don't do doesn't save us. Jesus has already done that for us.

4

DO I HAVE TO SAY AMEN?

Questions about the Bible, Prayer, and Religious Differences

Thanks to my parents and grandmother, my faith is so intertwined with early learning that I have trouble imagining the person I would be today without it. Stories of Bible characters shaped my own character from childhood. The prodigal son was the belligerent teenager living down the block in the big green house. Goliaths surrounded me as a scared first-grader picking her way to school. The feeding of the multitude on the hillside occurred every summer on vacation when my mother pulled out the egg salad sandwiches. God's loving me was no harder to believe than my grandmother's soft lap and bedtime stories.

When years later as a naive young English teacher I assumed a similar familiarity with Scripture on the part of high school students, I was in for a shock. While I was teaching *Grapes of Wrath*, I attempted an extended comparison of Steinbeck's Joad family and their trek to California with the Israelites and their exodus to the promised land. Repeatedly, the students looked baffled as I explained the parallel events and characters. Most had no more comprehension of these Old Testament personalities than I have of those from medieval Burmese literature.

As I pondered these huge gaps in the body of knowledge possessed by students in one of Minnesota's finest high schools, the words of Psalm 145 played through my memory: "One generation shall praise thy works to another." Plainly, after the mid-20th century, one generation had dropped the ball. Jesus' words, "When the Son of Man comes, will he find faith on earth?" echo through 2000 years and I think, "Well, will he?"

As parents we have Christ's command to transmit that faith to our children—not in complicated, wearisome lectures, but in the God-talk that speaks to our everyday existence. If our children are to grow up knowing God as someone who lives in people, not exclusively in a building, we need to make the Bible and prayer part of our everyday lives. Children are growing up with television, nuclear threats, and rock stars increasingly more "real" and more central to their lives than the knowledge and appreciation of God.

Kids are growing up confused because they hear parents telling them the Bible and prayer are important. But if they're important, often the children don't see *how*. The praying is often some hurried little ditty rattled off so as not to miss a favorite TV show. The revered Bible is picked up for Saturday cleaning or displayed when the pastor comes to visit.

Sometimes parents grow concerned about troubles that visit neighbors or relatives and riffle desperately through that same dusty book. They look for the magic verse that can protect them from disasters that may lurk in every encounter and decision. They seek the formula to make families immune from illness, poverty, and unhappiness. But the Bible does not exist for that purpose. With a few exceptions, the Bible does not picture many families on which we'd like to model our own.

The examples of Cain and Abel, Joseph and his envious brothers, Samuel handed over in infancy to an old priest who couldn't do a thing with his own sons, wily Jacob who tricked his blind father, the sons of David who raped and murdered their own sisters and brothers—these situations are more common than the happy domesticity for which we search the Scriptures.

Contrary to what many writers today are promulgating, the Bible was not written as a rule book for good marriages and stable families. Instead, it tells the sorrowful story of the brokenness and alienation that has plagued families and individuals since Adam and Eve chose to turn their back to God. And in chapter after chapter of Old and New Testament, we see bruised and bloodied people who no matter how hard they tried, couldn't find a good life by "living by the rules." For after all, if all we had to do to be good and happy was to follow rules, there would have been no need for that Child born in what was later called the Holy Family. There would have been no need for Jesus Christ, whose perfect obedience to his father and sacrificial love for us wins our salvation. Jesus provides the only model we need for our lives as individuals or in families.

Guidelines for sharing faith with children

1. When children are still infants, begin talking with them about how much God loves and cares for them. Tell them Bible stories of faithful people. Become involved in small and large Bible study groups through your congregation so that you yourself are thoroughly familiar with "the old, old story." Tell your children how "your story" interweaves with God's story, how your life has meaning and purpose because of Jesus. Read a book such as *Speaking in Stories* by William R. White (Augsburg, 1982) to give you a grasp of good storytelling technique.

2. Establish family rituals based on God's story. Your family might, for example, reenact the Passover or Seder meal yearly on Maundy Thursday, reliving the exodus of the Jews. How does the God of deliverance who led his people out of bondage in Egypt free us today? Talk about that with your family. The church year suggests many holy days or seasons that lend themselves to family ritual, Advent and Lent being the more obvious examples. Times such as vacations or trips to visit relatives can be used as the basis for family thanksgiving and prayers. A book you might find helpful along these lines is Darlene McRobert's *Family Fare* (Augsburg, 1981).

3. Make time for prayer every day. Teach your children both memorized and spontaneous prayer. Don't feel you must wait for bedtime or mealtime. As your children come to you—happy or sad, excited or bored—teach them from toddlerhood to share their feelings and experiences in prayer. Help them to grow up seeing prayer as a way of life. If spontaneous prayers seem too threatening at first for the family, ask them to write out brief prayers for meals or bedtime.

4. No matter how difficult it seems, find a few minutes a day for shared Bible reading. Rather than starting at Genesis and perhaps soon getting bogged down in dietary laws, use devotional helps, such as *Christ in Our Home*, that apply the daily Bible reading to everyday living in language all but the youngest children can understand. For a child's private devotional, you might look at *Pockets*, a periodical published by Upper Room. As you encourage family and personal Bible reading, help children not just to memorize Bible verses, but to incorporate them into daily living.

Questions about the Bible

Who wrote the Bible?

Many people wrote the Bible. The Bible is really many books combined into one. Around a thousand years went by during the time all of those books were being written and gathered into one.

Why is the Bible hard for me to understand?

Some parts are hard for adults to understand, too. Some parts are very easy. Since the Bible was written so long ago, many customs and ways of talking have changed and might seem strange to you. The important thing is to know the Bible tells us about Jesus.

Why do people call the Bible God's Word?

John 1:1 tells us that "In the beginning was the Word, and the Word was with God, and the Word was God." That refers to Jesus, the person at the center of the Bible. The Word of God comes to us in the Bible. It comes to us too as Christians speak of what God has done for us and what God's will is for us.

Is science or the Bible right?

The Bible tells us why God created the world. Scientists try to tell us how. So they can both be right. They answer different questions.

Why does the Bible have two parts?

The books of the Old Testament, the larger part, tell the story of God creating people and the world, how people became separated from God because of sin, and what God did to continue to show his love for people. The New Testament begins with the birth of Jesus, who was born to reunite us with God and goes on to tell of the early Christian church.

What's a gospel?

"The New Testament has four Gospels, the books of Matthew, Mark, Luke, and John that tell the *good news* of Jesus' birth, life, death, and resurrection. That's what *gospel* means— "good news."

What's an epistle?

Another word for epistle is *letter*. The epistles Paul wrote to different churches such as those in Rome and Corinth were letters to those congregations. In them, he and other writers gave advice and encouragement to the believers.

What's a testament?

A testament is a promise. That's what both testaments are about, God's promises to his people.

Why don't miracles happen anymore?

Who said miracles don't happen anymore? They don't happen often or we wouldn't call them miracles. A miracle means something very unusual, such as Jesus walking on water. But small miracles happen all the time if we look around. The way God's Spirit works in people, changing them to do God's will, is a miracle.

Do I have to read my Bible every day?

You don't have to read your Bible at all. But the more you read and know it, the more you will understand God's will for you.

Some parts of the Bible are boring. Do I have to read them?

Some chapters are hard to understand. If you read your Bible by yourself, you might read the Gospels, Epistles, and Psalms to begin with.

Does God talk to people now as he did in Bible days?

Sometimes we'd like guidance about matters the Bible doesn't speak about. We would like to hear God's voice booming loud and clear telling what to do and not to do. But God doesn't ordinarily appear to people today in the way he did to Moses. Still, through prayer and other believers, God's intentions for our lives can be learned.

Why are there different versions of the Bible?

The Old Testament was first written in Hebrew, and the New Testament in Greek. Different persons and groups worked hard to translate from those languages so people can have the Bible in their own language. Each time this has been done we've had another version. Some are better than others and closer to the original meaning. How sad it is, though, that many people don't read any version!

Questions about religious differences

What is a Jew? Did the Jews kill Jesus?

A Jewish person believes in one true God, just as Christians do. The difference is that Jews don't believe Jesus is truly the Son of God, the Messiah come to save us. It isn't fair to say Jews killed Jesus, because it was part of God's plan to die for everyone, and at first Jesus' followers were entirely Jewish. Jesus himself was a Jew.

What is a star of David?

Jewish people often wear an ornament called a star of David in the same way Christians sometimes wear a cross as a reminder of our faith.

Why do some churches baptize babies and others don't?

Many churches encourage parents to have their children baptized as infants. These churches believe Baptism is a sign of God's grace or free gift to us of Jesus. It is also a way of saying we are all helpless to do anything to save ourselves, that grownups are just as helpless as babies in the sight of God. Other churches teach Baptism is something that should be done when persons are old enough to decide if they want to live as Christians.

What is Passover?

If you read Exodus 11-12 you will learn about the first Passover meal. It is celebrated today by Jewish people, who remember that event when God saved his people from slavery. For Christians, it has an additional meaning. Jesus and his disciples were gathered to celebrate Passover the night before he was crucified, the night of the Last Supper. Jesus' dying for us was another way of saving us from slavery, this time the slavery of sin.

What is Hannukah?

This is a Jewish festival celebrated around the same time as Christmas. It's called the "Feast of Lights" and celebrates the rededication of the temple in Jerusalem shortly before Jesus was born.

How are Christians different from people of other religions?

In some ways we are the same as all believers. The important difference is that we believe we get to know God through Jesus Christ. Christians believe Jesus is God.

Why don't priests get married but most pastors do?

In some churches, mainly Roman Catholic, to be a priest you must make promises, including one that you won't marry. The idea is that you can then give yourself completely to being a good priest. Other churches believe clergy should be able to choose whether or not they want marriage and a family.

Why do Catholics pray to saints?

Not all Catholics do. Some believe people who led especially good lives on earth have more influence with God than do other people. Many Catholics pray to Jesus.

What is immersion?

Immersion is a way of baptizing when the whole body gets wet. Some churches baptize that way, others with a few drops of water. The important thing about Baptism is not the amount of water, but God's saving grace that happens in Baptism.

Why is the Lord's Supper called Eucharist in some churches?

Holy Communion, Lord's Supper, and Eucharist are some of the names given to the special time when believers eat and drink bread and wine as Jesus told us to do.

There's a boy in my class who can't salute the flag or go to parties because of his religion. Why?

He may belong to a group called Jehovah's Witnesses that believe people who salute the flag or have Christmas parties are not treating God respectfully.

Questions about prayer

Why do I need to pray? God knows what I'm thinking anyway.

Your parents probably know what your needs are too, but even so they want you to talk with them. Something very special happens when people pray that can't be easily explained.

What should I pray about?

Anything at all! You don't need big words. Whatever is on your mind is fine. Sometimes you might ask God for something. Other times, you might thank God for what he's done. We also need to confess our sins and pray for forgiveness.

If I pray, will I get what I ask for?

Sometimes. But God is not like a genie in a bottle who will grant you three wishes. Sometimes, because God loves you and wants what is best for you, you may not get what you ask for if it is harmful. That's because God has something better planned for you.

Does God always answer prayers?

Yes. Like a parent, sometimes God's answer is "yes," sometimes "no," and sometimes "later."

Does God hear my prayers?

Yes. Over and over the Bible tells us God wants us to pray to him and that he hears our prayers, even our silent ones.

Do I have to close my eyes?

You can pray anytime, anywhere. You don't need to kneel, or fold your hands, or close your eyes to talk to God. He is looking at our hearts more than what we are doing with our bodies.

Do I have to say Amen?

Not if you don't want to. "Amen" is the way we usually end our prayers because it says, "I really mean this."

5

DID THE DEVIL MAKE ME DO IT?

Questions about Evil, Sin, and Suffering

Sooner or later every child has an encounter with evil in this world. A vandal may have smashed a toy carelessly left on the sidewalk overnight. A pet may have been struck by a car in sight of the child who watched its death writhings in horror. Or a tornado may have devastated the neighborhood, leaving everyone numbed and unbelieving, and the child homeless. Sooner or later, no matter how heroically loving parents may try to shield the child, the unfair or evil realities of life intrude. "It's not fair!" a child may cry out in despair. "Why did this happen to me? Why did God let this happen?"

There are no easy answers to questions such as these. It will remain a mystery why a perfect and good God permits evil to exist in his universe. But we do catch a glimpse from the Bible of the reasons that trouble and tragedy can plague us.

First, the Scriptures repeatedly tell us God is good and made everything good. While the origin of evil is a question theologians may ponder, for children it is enough to know the truth of God's goodness.

Second, God created people with the freedom to obey or disobey God's will. And from the day of Adam to the present, people have often chosen disobedience. That disobedience or evil has brought sickness and death, selfishness and indifference to infect every part of our lives. But the story of salvation through the death and resurrection of Jesus tells us that "God was reconciling the world to himself in Christ" (2 Cor. 5:19). Jesus' resurrection won a permanent victory over evil.

Yet like isolated soldiers who have not yet heard that their side has surrendered and so continue their destructive skirmishing, evil continues to cause pain and turmoil in our lives. Why God does not make the world perfect now instead of waiting is something we want to know, but cannot. All we can do is trust, or in Buechner's words, "stand in the darkness and a hand is there, and we take it."

The greatest fear in the life of a young child is the unconscious terror of losing the love of parents or being separated from them. Love, order, and security are overwhelming needs. If a pet's life appears to be capriciously wiped out, if a beloved toy is broken for no apparent reason, the child's most basic fears of loss are intensified, because a child, even more than an adult, needs love and order for life to have meaning. As parents, we're challenged by the apparent randomness and meaninglessness of evil in the world as we try to impart to children the love, order, and security they so desperately need. We also realize we must build up our children's capacities to deal with life's inevitable crises and sorrows. We realize we can do this by giving them an unfailing sense of security. Children who grow up with such inner security are better equipped to handle the inevitable stresses and tumults of life as well as whatever catastrophes may lie in the future.

When disturbing events occur, encourage your child to ask for extra love and attention. Help the child to realize that God cares about everyone, and though evil things happen, God is still in charge.

With older children, you can begin to help them understand that out of evil and suffering can come the capacity for compassion. If we have had bad things happen to us, we can suffer with others. We can place ourselves for a time in the miserable or aching body of another. If we are compassionate, we feel another's pain in our own body. These are hard lessons, ones that children will not really learn for years. Many adults never have! But when we talk to our children about people such as St. Francis of Assisi, Albert Schweitzer, and Mother Teresa—people who've deliberately chosen to live among the suffering—we discover the beauty of spirit and Christlike sacrifice that suffering can draw from people.

Often people who are suffering are told, "It is God's will." This is an unfortunate way to try comforting someone, since it pictures God as selfish and cruel, visiting unhappiness and loss on his creatures. Explain instead to your child that we can follow God's direction through changing circumstances, even those coming out of evil. By following God's direction we help fulfill God's original plan—goodness and meaning for all people.

Some of the wisest words I've read about suffering come from another of Frederick Buechner's books, *Wishful Thinking:*

> God is all powerful. God is all-good. Terrible things happen.
>
> You can reconcile any two of these propositions with each other, but you can't reconcile all three. The problem of evil is perhaps the greatest single problem for religious faith.
>
> There have been numerous theological and philosophical attempts to solve it, but when it comes down to the reality of evil itself they are none of them worth much. When a child is raped and murdered, the parents are not apt to take much comfort from the explanation . . . that since God wants man to love him, man must be free to love or not to love and thus free to rape and murder a child if he takes a notion to.

Christianity . . . offers no theoretical solution at all. It merely points to the cross and says that, practically speaking, there is no evil so dark and so obscene—not even this—but that God can turn it to good.

Questions about evil and sin

What does the devil look like?

The Bible says the devil can disguise himself and take on any form, even an angel. The devil certainly doesn't run around in a red suit.

What is sin?

Sin is anything that separates us from God, or anything that is unloving to God or other people or even ourselves. Sin is anything hurtful or unloving.

Does the devil make me sin? I heard someone on TV say, "The devil made me do it!"

Many times people use the devil as an excuse for doing what they wanted to do themselves. The Bible tells us that we are tempted by the devil, the world around us, and from within ourselves. We are to resist that temptation no matter where it comes from.

Do all people sin? Even pastors?

You bet they do. Jesus is the only person who has ever lived who was sinless.

Why do people sin?

Every hurtful, mean thing we can do is caused by one thing: we love ourselves more than we love God. We want to do what we want, not what is loving and caring for God and others.

What is temptation?

Temptation is something bad or wrong that seems so good we want to do it even though we know we shouldn't.

How can I not give in to temptation?

You can pray for self-control, remind yourself that sooner or later you will be sorry you gave in and sinned. And you can get away from whatever it is that is tempting you. Don't make it harder on yourself than you have to!

How can I keep from sinning?

As long as you are a human being, you will continue to sin. But that doesn't mean you can't be forgiven for those sins. And you can and should pray to be strong to resist or avoid sin.

Do all sinners go to hell?

We are all sinners, so if heaven were only for nonsinners, no one would be there.

Why is it wrong to take candy from a store? There's plenty of it, and no one would miss it.

If you can take something from someone, then they should be able to take from you without your permission. You wouldn't like that, of course. The candy is the property of the person who owns the store, no matter how much candy there is.

If the clerk at the store gives me too much money back, is it all right to keep it?

The clerk's mistake does not make the money yours. If you were shortchanged, you'd probably mention it. If you get too much change, you should return it.

Why doesn't God make people be good?

God could have created people to be like puppets, only able to do what he tells them. But instead God made them with the ability to make choices. Much of the time we make wrong choices, ones that hurt ourselves and others. But God's Spirit working in us can help us to be more loving and kind.

Why does God let terrible things happen to people?

This is a hard question, and long books have been written asking the same thing. During recent years we have learned more about our world and have been able to prevent some of the accidents and diseases that used to kill more people. New inventions help us to know more about the weather and warn people that storms may be coming. God seems to have left a lot for us to learn, and maybe in the future people will use our ability to create more wisely. Still we will probably never understand everything about suffering while we live on this earth.

I prayed that grandpa would get well, but he died. Why didn't God make him well?

We don't know, but when you pray, it's important to ask God to do what is best, since we don't always know what the best thing is. God knew your grandpa's needs better than you could. Maybe he really wanted to go be with God.

What is the unforgivable sin? Have I done it?

A person who worries about committing the unforgivable sin would never have done it. According to the Bible, the unforgivable sin is forever turning your heart against the Holy Spirit. If you are thinking about this question, it means the Holy Spirit is working in you.

Why doesn't God kill off the bad people and let only the good ones live?

God is forgiving and patient, and keeps giving people the chance to repent and turn to him. God is more forgiving than any person we know.

Is it a sin to see X-rated movies [smoke, swear, drink, etc.]?

Anything that keeps us from loving God or being the kind of person God wants us to be is sin. For example, X-rated movies usually emphasize selfish, uncaring, and hurtful actions toward others. Watching them can encourage us to misuse God's gift of sexuality.

Is it a sin to be angry?

If anger is used to hurt people, it's wrong. When we feel angry—and we all do, sometimes—we need to express the anger. We should do it in ways, though, that don't hurt others. Talking about your anger to someone who cares about you, going outside and running for a while, or punching a pillow are some good ways you can deal with anger.

What is the worst sin?

God doesn't rate sins as "best" or "worst." Sin is sin, and we are all guilty, so it doesn't do much good to compare ourselves with someone we think might sin more than we do.

Who is Satan?

Satan is one of the names for the enemy of God, or the devil. Satan is the chief of all devils, and he wants to keep us from loving God and his people.

If God knows how bad I feel about what's happened, why doesn't he do something?

God has done something—two things, really. Two thousand years ago God was born as a human being—Jesus—and experienced suffering, pain, and death. So God knows how we feel. And today God provides other people who will care for us and love us when we feel bad.

If I try to be really good, will God always keep me safe and never let anything bad happen to me?

Some people say this is true, but the Bible says something else. It says that we may sometimes suffer for our faith. Peter says that since Christ suffered, we should be ready to suffer also (1 Peter 4:12-19).

What is a guardian angel?

The Bible talks about angels that guard our ways, to keep us from harm and various dangers. Luke 4 tells us about Jesus being tempted by the devil to take foolish chances because he had a guardian angel. Jesus answered by saying that we aren't supposed to put God to the test. That means God expects us to use common sense to stay out of trouble.

If I can't remember every sin when I pray for forgiveness, will God keep me from heaven?

People sin not only in what they do, but in what they don't do. We aren't even aware of much of our sin. So we can ask God to forgive not only the sins we remember, but also those we don't even know about.

No matter how hard I try to be good, I always end up doing bad. Why?

Paul, an early Christian who lived his whole life for the Lord, had the same problem. He said, "What I do is not the good I want to do; no, the evil I do not want to do—this I keep on doing" (Rom. 7:19). All Christians have a daily struggle with evil in their lives. We need forgiveness and the Holy Spirit working in us every day to help us be more like Jesus.

6

WHEN I GROW UP
CAN I MARRY DADDY?

Questions about Marriage, Divorce, and Remarriage

It's one of the signs of the times that the day I sat down to write this chapter, I noticed in our daily newspaper the list of divorces was longer than the list of marriage licenses granted. In a country where one in two marriages is estimated to end in divorce, it seems appropriate that a book about answering children's questions relating to faith and the world deal with topics that a few generations ago would not have been included: divorce and remarriage. The hard truth is that Christians are not immune to the breakdown of marriage, and many separated and divorced Christian parents face heartbreaking questions from their children. The prevalence of divorce today means many children grow up assuming that eventually their parents' marriage too will end that way. If most of their friends' parents have been divorced, it's a natural assumption. It just happens after a while, they think.

This is sad. While we realize God did not create people for marriage, but rather marriage for human blessing, society today trivializes marriage by encouraging divorce. As Christians, however, we cannot take lightly the Bible's comparison of marriage with Christ and the church, his body. It is through happy marriages and the commitment married persons show each other that the child can most easily learn of God's faithfulness. Through the give-and-take, trust and forgiveness, reconciliation and affirmation of marriage, a child catches a glimpse of what the Christian life is like. Since it is primarily from parents that children learn their view of God, what will they know of God's faithfulness and abiding love if parents casually disregard their marriage vows? Or what will it mean to live in a trusting faith relationship with God?

Nobody said it would be easy, and these days it seems to be harder than ever to maintain a happy marriage. Perhaps it's that we have higher expectations than did our grandparents. Whatever the case, it's important that we teach our children that a happy marriage is a blessing, a gift of grace. As with other attitudes, what our children see modeled is more effective than what they are told.

Nevertheless, after a period of soul-searching and prayer, many Christian parents come to the conclusion that to stay married is not right for them or for the child. For believers put in the position of having to explain to children why mommy and daddy aren't living together any more, separation and divorce must be an even more heartwrenching experience.

Since no one knows what any other person may be suffering, it's judgmental and unnecessary to make critical comments about the breakup of another's marriage. Thank God if yours is happy, and pray for guidance that it may continue to be so.

Younger children's questions about marriage

Mothers and fathers are sometimes shocked to learn that preschoolers may intend to marry the parent of the opposite sex when they grow up. Child development experts know this to be a stage most children go through. Psychiatrists refer to the strong attraction of the child to the parent of the opposite sex as the "Oedipal phase," after King Oedipus of Greek mythology who killed his father and married his mother. While this attraction is common, it's important that parents not encourage such fantasies, stated or not.

Can I marry daddy when I grow up?

When you grow up, you'll find a special person you want for your husband. Daddy is my husband, and although he'll always love you, he'll love you as a father, not a husband.

In the following exchange, notice how the parent reassures the child while at the same time reminding him of his place in the family.

"Mommy, I really love you. Do you love me?"

"Sure, I love you Jason. You're very special to me."

"Yeah, but you love dad, too."

"Yes, I do."

"Why don't you divorce him?"

"We don't want a divorce. We want to stay married and both love and care for you."

People such as Art Linkletter have delighted audiences by asking questions of children concerning marriage and family. Their amusing answers illustrate the problems children have with abstract ideas. A wedding is an event to which they can relate, but a marriage, a relationship, can be understood only in terms of the people they know who are "in marriage," the words of a four-year-old.

What is marriage?

A man and a woman promise before God to love each other and be very special to each other until one of them dies. When they are married the man is called a husband; the woman, a wife.

How will I know whom to marry?

You will meet someone you love very much, a person who loves you too. You will want to be special to each other and to live together forever.

Do I have to get married?

No one has to get married. Some people choose not to. They too can have happy lives.

Older children's questions about marriage

Can you love someone and still argue?

I know you heard mom and me arguing. People who love each other very much don't always agree about everything, and we were working out a disagreement. We compromised, and everything's OK now. That's part of being married— working out disagreements.

Are two people "meant for each other"? What if I don't find the right one?

Sometimes books or movies give us the idea that for every person there is a perfect mate, and you will fall in love at first sight when you meet that person. Actually, there are probably many people with whom you could have a happy marriage. The important thing is that when you find the person you want to marry, you remain faithful.

Younger children's questions about divorce

Young children whose parents are going through divorce are often unable to voice the questions that plague them. At the same time, the parents may be feeling so much anger and pain they are scarcely able to be sensitive to the needs and unspoken questions of their children. Children may then turn to teachers, grandparents or others for help. It's important that they get answers, for therapists agree that those children who receive reasonable explanations are far better able to handle their grief and confusion.

It may be of some comfort to divorced parents to learn that children's reaction to divorce is almost universal and often follows a pattern. Shock, depression, denial, anger, shame, and guilt usually beset the child, often in that order, along with fantasizing about ways to reunite the parents. The child may feel as though his or her whole world is falling apart. Preschoolers have trouble comprehending that both parents will no longer be there when needed and wanted, and may feel abandoned. To help children through this difficult time, it's wise for parents to consider the following:

1. How will we prepare the child? What will we say? Some parents take a cowardly way out of this by saying nothing. Father may just disappear, then suddenly show up for a visit some weekend. In the meantime, without some explanation, the child may assume the father has died or magically disappeared. Experts agree that no matter how young, the child must be given some explanation, if possible, by both parents.

2. Are we being honest without burdening the child with too many intimate and unnecessary details?

3. Are we helping the child to feel he or she will not lose the love of either parent, even though one will be living elsewhere (or in the case of desertion, explaining that the absent parent did not leave the family because of the child)?

4. Do we refuse to put the child in a position of taking sides? If one parent blames the other, the child will feel more torn and confused. Name-calling only invites the child to come to the defense of the parent being run down.

Children of divorced parents learn at an early age what is safe or unsafe to admit. The child whose mother feels furious and betrayed by her ex-husband will quickly learn not to confess missing the father for fear of the mother's rage. The longing for father may be bottled up, pushed down, while at the same time anger grows at the mother for putting the child into that position. The anger toward the mother can't be mentioned, however, because in a small child's mind, acknowledging that anger might mean the mother will leave too.

As these issues are considered, remember that divorce is not easily comprehended by small children. It may be necessary to give repeated reassurances that the child will be cared for and loved. It's a good idea to tell the child you welcome questions and to reflect his or her confusion and sadness. "You're still feeling mixed up, aren't you, Janie? That's OK. We can talk about it if you'd like."

What is a divorce?
A divorce means mom and I won't be living in the same house anymore.

Why are you getting a divorce?
For a long time we haven't been able to get along with each other. We think everyone will be happier if we live separately.

Will you divorce me?
Daddy and I aren't angry with you. Only married people get divorces. Both of us will continue to love you. It's important you know that.

Who will take care of me?
You still have a mother and you still have a father. You will be living with your mother [or father] but you will see your father [or mother] often. There will always be someone who will take care of you and love you.

If mommy really loves me, why is she going away?
I wish I could tell you. She isn't going because of anything you did or didn't do. It's because she isn't happy with me. But she still loves you and we will both take care of you. We won't be living in the same house to do that.

If I'm really good, will daddy come back and live with you?
Daddy didn't leave because of anything you did or didn't do. He left because we aren't getting along. Your being good won't change that.

Older children's questions about divorce

By the ages of eight to twelve, children have become somewhat familiar with what's involved in divorce. Many of their friends' parents may be divorced. At the same time, older children may be somewhat more reluctant than younger ones to verbalize the questions that deeply concern them. Although they are not asking these questions, they may be wondering about their part in the divorce and what will happen to them. Questions not asked only go underground, where fantasy and distortion can cause more problems. It's crucial to encourage the child to express feelings and ask questions: "I've noticed, Bobby, that you haven't had much to say since I told you about the divorce. I'm sure you must have some questions. I'll do my best to answer them for you."

Preadolescent children have a very strict, almost rigid, sense of right and wrong. When the parent who has taught the rules does not, in the child's opinion, keep those rules, the child may become resentful. Divorcing parents are often neatly labeled as "the good one" and "the bad one." Parents who really care about the child's welfare more than their own desire for revenge will do what they can to minimize this attitude.

Depending on the sensitivity of the child and other factors, such as the amount of time spent with the noncustodial parent, a certain amount of regression in behavior can be expected. It is not uncommon to see whining and difficulty in going to sleep among children who haven't acted that way in years. Children may have trouble concentrating in school. An unverbalized fear of abandonment is probably at the root of these behaviors. "After all," the child may feel, "if mom promised to love dad but changed her mind about him, how do I know she won't change her mind about me?" Reassuring older children that mom or dad will be around to love and care for them is as necessary as with very young children.

What about the parent who deserts the family, showing no

intention of keeping in touch with the child? What does the caregiving parent say in such a case? Obviously, it's dishonest to pretend the situation is similar to a divorce in which both parents love and continue to care for the child. When months go by without a phone call or visit or support check, the child should get a kind but truthful explanation, one in which the justifiably angry parent does not berate the absent one. A realistic answer to the child's questions, voiced or unvoiced, is the best idea. "I don't understand either why your father acts as he does, David. It hurts me, and it hurts you. But I promise that I will always be here to take care of you, and your dad isn't staying away because of anything you've done."

Painful as it may be, the truth will help the child get on with life. Help the child to understand that people are not all good or all bad, and we don't know everything that goes on inside a person that causes irresponsible behavior.

What did you fight about?

We fought about money [or drinking, or dad's staying out late]. (It's not necessary or advisable to go into detail. In many cases, it might be better to say, "That's something very personal. There are things you want to keep private, and this is one of those things I don't care to talk about. I'll try to answer most of your questions, though.")

What did I do to make her leave us?

Mom isn't leaving because of you. She isn't leaving to punish you. We have thought about this and decided it will be best for the whole family in the long run.

What did you do to make her leave us?

(This can be a painful question for the parent who considers the guilt to lie on the other partner's side. At the same time, the child may be striking out at the available parent, making that one a target for the child's own anger and hurt. The child may feel that somehow, some way, the remaining parent should have been able to hold the marriage together.)

It wasn't something either one of us did. We both made mistakes. We both feel bad about what happened.

My friend says divorce is a sin. Is it?

God intended that when people get married, they stay married, because that's usually best for everyone. But sometimes people find out they shouldn't have been married and get a divorce. When that happens, God forgives that sin just as he forgives every other sin. God feels bad when any of his children, your size or my size, hurt inside.

Who will play ball with me [fix my hair, etc.]?

You'll still be seeing your dad. When you get together weekends, you can have fun doing those special things. In between times, I'll try to play ball with you, too. Moms can do things with their kids they don't always do when the other parent is around. I'll be learning some new skills now that dad isn't living with us.

Will I get divorced some day too?

I hope not. I hope you don't make the same mistakes your dad and I made. A good marriage is a wonderful gift from God, and there are many people who are able to have that kind of marriage. Your dad and I just weren't able to.

What will happen if you die and dad doesn't want me to live with him?

The chances are very small that I won't live till you're grown up and able to live by yourself. And if it should ever be that you couldn't live with your dad, either, we have asked Aunt Janet to take care of you. I'm sure that won't happen, but you need to know that there will always be someone around to love and care for you till you're grown.

What will we do for money?

Dad will send a check every month. (Or,) I'm going back to work. We won't have as much money as we did, but we'll have plenty to eat so don't worry about that.

What will my friends think?

They won't think any less of you because mom and I are getting a divorce. That's between us. You can say we weren't happy and we thought everyone would be better off if we didn't live together anymore. Or you don't have to say anything if you don't want to. If someone asks, just say you don't want to talk about it.

About remarriage

Divorce is never easy for children. At the same time, God gave them a remarkable ability to spring back, to withstand even the most traumatic of events. If at the time of divorce, a parent—or better yet, both parents—can give the child understanding, warmth, and answers, the child will undoubtedly weather the crisis. Psychologists have discovered that in every child there exists a drive toward good health and well-being. With help from parents, the child will move in this direction and be prepared for what is often the next period of adjustment, the parents' remarriage.

When I was three years old, my widowed mother remarried. To my great joy, I then had a living father, an adoptive father who loved me as dearly as he later loved the three daughters born to him and my mother. Now, after many years, though, I can still remember the rage and indignation I felt as a child when people referred to my new daddy as my "stepfather." How *dare* they call him that, this father who adopted me and treated me as his own?

I relate these feelings because now, years later, the same stigma of "stepparents" remains, perhaps to a lesser degree, but still present. Children's literature—*Cinderella, Hansel and Gretel, Snow White,* for a few examples—sometimes perpetuates the idea of stepparents as being cruel and vicious. In stories like these stepchildren take second place, if any at all, in the stepparents' affections. To many, "stepchild" connotes neglect or disfavor. Is it any wonder that the divorced parent's remarriage looms as an adjustment often greater than the divorce?

Stepparents often feel as though they have been placed in a no-win situation. With the remarriage, the child's secret hope that someday the original parents will get back together has been dashed. Often the stepparent is seen unrealistically as an interloper, someone who has come between the child's natural parents. Old feelings of fear and guilt may be resurrected. Because of this, the stepparent who envisions the child of the previous marriage as rushing into his or her arms is probably doomed to disappointment. In most cases, love for the stepparent is won inch by hard-earned inch by repeatedly demonstrating love and caring for that child. Having already been hurt, many children are wary of the new parent, a person who seems to receive too much affection from the original parent.

This may seem discouraging to someone planning to become a stepparent, but it would be unfair to lead anyone to think this new set of relationships often comes easily. New, combined families *can* be successfully established, however, and some actions and statements smooth this difficult period.

1. Gradual preparation for the coming marriage is the best course. Too often the relationship is rushed, and the child is overwhelmed with attention or gifts designed to win favor for the prospective parent. Too much hugging and excessive interest may threaten the child, well-meant though they be, and the attempt can backfire. Without understanding why, the child may reject or disdain the advances of the stepparent-to-be, in turn causing withdrawal and confusion on the part of

the adult. The best policy seems to be to show patience and interest, and only as the child appears ready, to increasingly show signs of affection.

A great deal of "wooing" and special treatment of the child is not advisable for another reason. It may encourage the child to feel a sense of power verging on control. The decision about remarriage belongs with the parents, not the child or as the result of a "majority vote."

2. Besides the child's mixed feelings (assuming some good ones exist) another factor is important in the remarriage situation: jealousy toward the former mate. Many stepfathers confess they can hardly bear hearing their children speak admiringly of natural fathers, and stepmothers likewise often resent hearing about the virtues of the mothers who preceded them. If a stepparent honestly did admit to the new spouse these feelings, much tension might be forestalled. At the same time, this jealousy might make it easier to empathize with the child who is also feeling jealous of the new person taking so much of the natural parent's attention and time.

3. Treat natural and stepchildren equally. This seems obvious, but it's easier said than done. Many stepparents, trying hard to avoid the accusation of favoritism toward their natural children, go overboard in permissiveness to stepchildren, thereby alienating their own. Be as consistent and fair as you can possibly be.

Some questions about remarriage

Why do you have to marry somebody else? Why don't you just marry dad again if you want to be married?

We want to be married because we love each other and want to be together. I don't want just to be married, I want to be married to this particular person.

Will I still be able to see mom after you get married?

Yes, your mother will always be your mother, and you'll still be able to see her. No one is ever going to take the place of your mother.

Are you going to be our new dad?

I'll be your mom's husband. I won't be your father, but I do want to have a good relationship with you. You'll still have your dad as your father.

Do I have to call you dad?

Dad is what you call your father. That's a special name for him. You can experiment with different nicknames for me or call me by my first name. (Some experts think stepparental authority is undermined by use of first names. Others think what the stepparent is called is not nearly as important as the underlying quality of the relationship. Decide what you feel comfortable with and talk about it with the child.)

You're not my mom. Why do I have to do what you say?

I know you feel I don't belong here, but I honestly care about you and want what's best for you. Your father and I both expect you to obey me as well as him.

Who will I spend Christmas with—mom or dad?

(Probably at no other time except weddings or funerals do the problems of combined families surface more regularly than at holidays. These times which should be so happy are often filled with tension. One method that seems to work for some families is to have the child alternate holidays between the two homes. The decisions you make may seem unorthodox, but if they offer solutions, stay with them. Talk over arrangements ahead of time. Leave as little as possible to chance.)

Building a new life isn't easy. But with encouragement, openness and answers given truthfully and sympathetically, combined families can be happy families.

7

WHERE DID I COME FROM?

Questions about Sexuality and Adoption

When a little boy asked his mother where he'd come from, his mother drew a deep breath before launching into a lengthy technical explanation of the reproductive process. When at last she finished, she asked her son, "There, do you have any questions?"

The little boy looked up at her, confusion written all over his face. "Mom, I meant, did we move here from Chicago or Milwaukee?"

Many parents can tell similar stories documenting how their own children have elaborated, simplified, or fantasized on the facts of life which have been carefully presented to them. Why do most parents have such a difficult time communicating ideas about sexuality to children, either going overboard with too much unasked-for information like the mother in the anecdote, or on the other hand, sidestepping questions with evasions and fairy tales?

Adults feel uncertain and uncomfortable presenting sexual information for many reasons. They may worry that they can't be effective teachers, especially if they did not themselves receive sex education in their homes but on the street. Sometimes parents believe they will confuse and frighten their children by telling too much too soon, or wonder how they can possibly explain such a complex subject as adult sexual motivation and behavior. Most of all, they may fear that children who know about sex will practice it.

This chapter will attempt to help parents answer questions both asked and left unspoken, and suggest ways to help teach positive attitudes toward sexuality and love.

Parents, after all, begin unconsciously to do just that—teach about sexuality—when the child is born. When you hold your baby to your breast at birth, when you feed, cuddle and caress the infant, you begin teaching that psychological intimacy is safe and good. You begin to teach that personal involvement is something to be desired. The children with whom I work have largely been deprived of that psychological intimacy as babies and now find real closeness too threatening. In early adolescence such children often turn their real need for love into counterfeit relationships based on physical sex. They have not yet learned that physical intimacy is alienating without psychological intimacy—without commitment, responsibility, and tenderness. These teenagers may understand some of the mechanics of sex, but they don't comprehend personal integrity, dignity, or privacy. These children represent only a few human statistics from the sobering numbers with which social workers are all too familiar.

Close to 1.5 million known teenage pregnancies annually and 2 million new cases of sexually transmitted diseases a year among adolescents tell us that today's young people don't "know it all." In spite of today's permissive society and explicit films and language, many children are growing up not knowing what is really important about sexuality. The question for parents is not, shall my child have sex education, but, from whom will it be learned? Will it be learned from the media or peers?

Such education generally portrays sex in a depersonalized, trivial manner. It implies casual sexual relationships that use other people are not only acceptable but even desirable. It makes sex education into a how-to course rather than one that emphasizes values and relationships.

If you are the type of parent who has shown affection and encouraged high self-esteem in your child, you have made a good beginning. After all, teaching about sexuality does not mean lecturing three-year-olds with clinical descriptions. It does mean parents realize they are constantly sending messages about sex, whether they say anything or not. By the time children are five or six, they have already developed feelings and viewpoints about their bodies and how men and women relate to each other. Whether those attitudes are positive or negative depends largely on the parents' own attitudes, as well as their understanding some of the confusions that exist in children's minds regarding sexuality. What are some of these misconceptions?

Gender identity

By the age of two or three, most children are aware of gender. Your son identifies with the label "boy" although he may have no idea of the physical and social connotations of maleness. At this age gender is not determined by genital differences but rather clothing, hair styles, and behavior. ("Gender" is social, whereas "sex" is biological.)

Since two of your child's earliest words are probably "boy" and "girl," it's easy to think the essential differences are understood long before this is the case. When our Katie was about two, she referred for over a year to her three-year-old brother Erik as "Boy" in place of his name. "Boy" to her meant not any young male, but rather a specific person. Until children are five or six, they are uncertain as to whether gender can change. And although they are aware that infants somehow emerge from mommies, the role of daddies in the process is unclear to them.

Vocabulary difficulties

Because old words used in new ways—*egg* and *seed* for example—tend to confuse children, parents' attempts to explain reproduction in these terms is often less than helpful. I remember one mother's story of her five-year-old's asking how the baby got inside the mother. She answered by saying that when a mommy and daddy love each other a lot, the daddy plants a seed in the mommy and it grows into a baby. A few days later, she was puzzled to see her son examining his young sister's navel. "I put some birdseed in there yesterday, but nothing's growing yet," he reported. "Are you sure that's how the baby gets there?"

Another vocabulary problem, probably not as prevalent now as formerly, is the tendency to leave unnamed the parts of the body "down there." When euphemisms such as "bottom" are always used, children might assume that places which can't be named must be bad or dirty.

In early elementary years it's common to find children experimenting with gutter language overheard at school, taking a sniggering delight in using forbidden words, words for which you may have carefully taught acceptable equivalents. How should this be handled? Most experts agree that punishment is often not effective in handling such experiments in obscenity. (I myself can remember the effect on my mouth when brown laundry soap was used the time I tried out such a new word.) You might ask the child if he or she knows the meaning of the word or phrase and if not, explain what it means. Tell you child that such language is offensive and unpleasant to others.

Magic versus cause and effect

Until children reach the age of six or seven, they tend to see little relationship between cause and effect. They tend instead to believe in a fantasy/fact combination of causal events. You're likely to get a different answer to your question about how people get babies from each child who's asked. Few mention the stork or cabbage patch anymore, but nevertheless, many misconceptions are there. One child described the baby as being put together "some place" and then brought to the hospital where it was put in the mother. On further questioning, the child revealed a point of view of "mother-as-oven." Like a loaf of bread, the baby was assembled in one place and then placed in the mother for finishing. Frequently such ideas are not obvious to parents who don't go out of their way to find out what their child might be thinking.

While these misunderstandings may be amusing among small children, they can cause serious problems for teenagers. How many cases of pregnancy and venereal disease, I wonder, have occurred because adolescents have not been given correct information or acquired positive attitudes about themselves. Girls have expressed numbed amazement upon finding that yes, they really could become pregnant "the first time." Some of the misconceptions about sex held by our worldly teenagers would be funny if the results were not so upsetting or dangerous.

Guidelines for teaching sexuality

1. Determine the meaning of your child's question. Before you answer, ask for your child's opinion. If a child thinks a baby rests in the mother's body alongside the food she's just eaten, it's easy for the child to think the same situation is possible for himself. Once you find out what is really the question and what your child's fantasies are, you're more likely to give a helpful answer.

2. Don't give more information than needed. Answer only the specific question you think is really being asked. If you answer in such a way that your child knows you are willing to answer, the child will be there to ask the next time more information is needed.

3. Talk in terms of people and relationships. Most of children's questions don't apply to animals or abstractions. If answers to sexual questions deal only with reproduction, children believe people have intercourse only when they "make babies." When you frame your answers in terms of a marriage relationship, you help children see sexuality not just as something that is done, but as a part of personhood.

4. Be aware that you are teaching values as you answer questions. When a child who has been listening to older children asks you to explain how homosexuals "do it," your values will be heard louder than what you actually say. If disgust or horror are perceived by the children when certain questions are asked, further questioning is effectively ended.

5. Encourage children to ask questions. Children don't get to be very old without realizing sexual questions raise parental anxiety level in a way most other questions never do. Because of this, they may stop asking parents and look to other sources of information. (By adolescence they almost always do this.) If your young children haven't been asking many questions, you might casually bring up the subject.

Depending on the age of your child, an event such as seeing a very pregnant woman could open a conversation. A comment such as "That woman looks like I did just before you were born," might open up the topic for some questions on the topic the child has been avoiding with you.

6. Build high self-esteem. The children who turn to sexual relationships in early adolescence do so largely because they crave approval and affection. Teens who have received plenty of both from early childhood at home rarely get involved in

premature sexual relationships. They have a sense of self-worth that enables them to withstand the strong social pressures they know to be wrong. Along with plenty of love and affection, teaching them what you believe to be right and wrong in the area of sexuality strengthens self-esteem.

About adoption

With the exception of questions specifically sexual in nature, probably few other topics can be as unsettling as adopted children's questions about adoption. Nonadoptive parents have trouble understanding the extent to which adoptive parents have been forced to examine issues such as infertility, undesirable genetic traits that might "contaminate" adopted children, unwed parenthood, and a fear of natural parents somehow showing up to claim their child—to name only a few. While their child is still an infant, adoptive parents often express concern about how they'll explain adoption. How will they explain what happened in a way the natural parents are seen in a positive light, not as monsters who abandoned their unwanted child?

Adoptive parents may fear that their child will later desire to be reunited with natural parents, parents the child fantasizes are somewhere waiting desperately for her. In the fantasy they are perfect parents, unlike the ordinary folks with whom the child lives and of whose shortcomings he or she is all too aware.

Don't make adoption central to your child's being. Constantly reminding the child of being "special" because of adoption can be anxiety-producing or embarrassing, especially when the child is introduced as "Peter, our special, adopted son."

Many suggestions for teaching about sexuality apply also to the topic of adoption. Being neither evasive nor verbose when questions are asked and determining what is really being asked are both important.

As is the case with many other types of questions, the more adults understand and care about the needs and concerns of children at various ages, the more sensitively will they be able to answer them.

Questions about sexuality from preschoolers

Where do babies come from?

A special place inside the mother.

That lady is fat. Is a baby in her stomach?

No, the baby grows in a special pocket women have that is called a uterus.

Did she swallow something?

No, the baby is growing inside her.

How did the baby get in the mother?

Part of the mother and father came together and the baby grew inside the mother's uterus.

How does the baby come out?

Through a special opening between the mother's legs. (If the child wants more information, add, "It's not the same opening as for urinating or a bowel movement." Many kids confuse reproductive and digestive processes.)

Can a baby grow in me?

Only grown women can have babies grow in them.

Why can't daddies have babies?

Daddies help the mothers have babies. Without part of the father joining with the part from the mother, there wouldn't be a baby.

What are the parts called?

The mother's part is called an egg or ovum. The father's part is called the sperm.

How big are they? Is the egg like a chicken egg?

The egg is about the size of the dot on an *i*. The sperm is even smaller. You can't see one without a microscope.

Do you make a boy baby different from a girl baby?

All babies are made from the mother's part and the father's part joining together. Usually the parents don't know until the baby is born whether it's a boy or girl.

Why don't I have a penis?

All boys have penises. All girls have vaginas. That's the way they were born.

Questions asked by elementary-age children

Unlike preschoolers, children aged 6-10 can understand that a world existed before they were born, that events have causes, and that time is needed for certain processes such as pregnancy. They may often ask questions previously asked, but at this age are ready for more detailed answers. From television and school friends they have heard about topics such as rape, abortion, and homosexuality. If you've been open in answering earlier questions, they will bring up these or other unsettling topics.

How do people get babies?

When a husband and wife love each other and want to have a baby, the husband puts his penis into the wife's vagina. Sometimes, but not always, the sperm from the father's penis joins with the ovum or egg inside the mother. That's the beginning of a baby. It takes nine months to grow inside the mother before it's born.

Do people always get babies when they do that?

No. Husbands and wives like being close in this special, grown-up way. This way of showing love is called "making love" or "sexual intercourse." Husbands and wives make love when they want to please each other, not only when they want a baby.

Do you have to be married to have a baby?

No. Anytime a man and a woman have sexual intercourse, it's possible that a baby can begin. That's one of the reasons that God wants the special kind of grown-up love to happen between married people. That way there are two parents to care for a baby if the woman has one. A baby needs lots of care and love, and it's much easier for two people who love each other to provide that attention.

How does a woman know if she's going to have a baby?

If she has had sexual intercourse and thinks she might be pregnant, a doctor can examine her and tell if she's pregnant.

Is the baby growing in the mother's stomach? How does it grow bigger?

The baby grows near the stomach in a special place called the uterus. The baby grows inside a water bag that protects it. A cord called the umbilical cord connects the baby and mother and gives the baby food and air from the mother.

How do you know when the baby is ready to come out?

The mother feels muscles around the baby tighten up. The uterus pushes the baby out through the mother's vagina.

Does it hurt?

Often it does, but mothers and fathers can learn to work to help the baby come more easily. When the baby is born they are so happy they forget any discomfort.

What happened to my cord?

The doctor cut it when you were born and no longer needed it. The scar is called your navel.

What does a uterus look like?

An upside down pear or balloon. It's small when the woman is not pregnant, but can grow very large to hold the growing baby. After the baby is born, it shrinks back like a balloon after the air is let out.

Why do women have large breasts and men small ones?

God gave women breasts to feed their babies from. When a baby is born, milk is formed in women's breasts. After the baby stops nursing, or if the mother feeds her baby with a bottle instead, there is no more milk, but women's breasts stay larger than men's anyway.

How do the eggs and sperm get into people's bodies?

When people reach their teens, their bodies manufacture them. The woman's eggs that are inside her begin to be ready to grow a baby. The man's sperm begins to be produced in his scrotum, the bag that hangs between his legs.

Questions asked by older children

Prior to the onset of adolescence, children's questions become more related to themselves and the body changes that they've begun to see occurring. They're incredibly sensitive to peer influence, and parents may be dismayed to have their own influence lessening and values questioned. Now, more than ever before, the child's self-esteem or lack of it will affect sexuality. A girl who matures very early can be flattered yet uneasy about the sudden attention from boys who shortly before didn't know she existed. A boy may be increasingly aware and confused because of a double standard in society, one that may be at odds with what you've taught him about morality.

Experts suggest that you teach girls about menstruation and boys about erections and wet dreams before the age of ten.

You can be sure that by that age they have already picked up misinformation from friends. As children head into the tumultuous teens, it's more important than ever that parents do more listening and less lecturing.

The pressures are tremendous on teenagers and appear to be intensifying to have an early sexual initiation. Cases of pregnancy among 12- and 13-year-old girls are no longer rare. Just the other evening my eighth-grade son talked about a girl in his class who's pregnant. When I asked him where he'd heard this, his answer came quickly. "Everybody knows about it except her mother." His mention of this sad news was an opportunity for a discussion about the sense of responsibility that should be a part of sexual behavior, and the chances of a marriage succeeding with an eighth-grade bride and a ninth-grade groom.

Other topics that should be dealt with as the child nears adolescence is the way both boys and girls manipulate the opposite sex and use them sexually and why marriage, with its commitment, is the setting in which God intended sexual intercourse.

When will I start having periods?
Most girls begin their menstrual periods sometime between the ages of 11 and 14.

What does it mean to have a period?
Girls are born with two ovaries, each containing hundreds of eggs. When you begin to menstruate, you know that each month one of those tiny eggs leaves the others and goes into a Fallopian tube near the uterus. The part of the monthly cycle you call your period is when the uterus gets rid of the lining it prepared in case the egg was fertilized and a baby started.

How will I know if I have a period?
You will notice a stain on your underwear. It means the

lining that contains blood is coming out of the uterus through the vagina.

Does the blood just pour out?
No, it begins slowly, and you have time to use some protection so you don't have an accident.

How do you go to the bathroom when you have a period?
Your menstrual blood comes from the vagina, not the place you urinate or have a bowel movement.

What makes my penis get hard?
A penis is filled with blood vessels. When they fill up with blood, it gets hard and is called an erection. Boys and men get erections for many reasons, from being scared or cold or having to go to the bathroom. When you're older, sexual excitement will make an erection.

What happens when a man has an erection?
Many times it just goes away, like goosebumps when you're no longer cold. Sometimes a fluid called semen comes out of the penis.

What is a wet dream?
When a man or boy is sleeping and has an erection, the semen can come out without his knowing what happened. It's normal and nothing to be frightened or ashamed of.

Will I go blind if I touch myself? My grandma said I would.
Many times in the past children were told this could happen. What you're referring to is called masturbation, and it doesn't cause anyone to go blind.

Why do people have intercourse?
God gave people the urge to make love as a way of keeping the human race going. It's very enjoyable when done with

someone you love and trust. I believe God meant intercourse for married people as a special way of showing how much they love each other.

How long does it take?

It can take a few minutes or sometimes longer.

Can you do something so a baby doesn't get started?

Yes. Either the man or woman or both can prevent a baby from beginning. It's called birth control.

Questions about adoption

Did I come from your tummy?

You came from a mother's body, but I didn't become your mother until after you were born.

Why didn't my birth parents keep me?

Maybe they were so young themselves when you were a baby that they didn't know how to give you the care and attention you needed, so they made sure you'd get that love by letting you be adopted. We wanted a child very much and were able to care for you, so that's how you came to be part of our family.

Where did you go to adopt me?

(Explain how arrangements were made through the agency or whatever means were used.)

Sometimes I feel bad because I can't remember my first mom and dad. Is that bad?

You probably can't remember many things that happened to you when you were very small. It's OK.

Do people really pick out the child they want, like in a store?

Not usually, at least with our agency. Sometimes people know the exact child they will adopt, but usually they are surprised like any other new parents.

(Don't tell your child he was chosen because he was the best. Unless it was an extremely unusual adoption, it's just not true, and puts unrealistic expectations on that child. He'll feel he has to constantly keep measuring up to being the "most chooseable one.")

Do you love me more [or less] than my brothers and sisters who weren't adopted?
You're all equal in our hearts. It doesn't matter if you were born or adopted into our family; we feel the same about you.

If I get angry at you, can I go back to my birth mother?
No. You are our child forever and ever.

How did my birth mother feel when she gave me away?
(Answer this question as empathically as possible from the birth mother's point of view. Emphasize the fact that the mother's relinquishment was her decision and had nothing to do with your child's goodness or badness. Explain her decision in the context of being done for the child's welfare.)

Why do you call yourself my father? You're not my real father!
Yes, I am your real father. You didn't start from my body, but we have taken care of you, and now I am your real and true father. Even if you're angry with me, I'm still your father.

8

WHY DID GRANDMA DIE?

Questions about Death and Eternal Life

Experts have suggested that death has taken the place of sex as being the subject about which parents are most uncomfortable in discussing with their children. Some parents who are careful to avoid euphemisms when they talk to their children about sexual matters resort to all kinds of evasions in speaking about death: "Grandma is only sleeping," or "Your dog passed away last night." Other parents shield the child from the knowledge of death by suggesting the person who died "went on a long trip." Because many parents are afraid of traumatizing or threatening their children, they are quick to do what they can to spare children the realities of grief, sorrow, and loss. Undoubtedly some of this is due to adults' reluctance to deal with their own mortality.

Most child care experts believe it's wrong to deprive the child of the natural and profound emotions that accompany death. Death is part of the life cycle, and to pretend it doesn't exist is to make life itself superficial. Certainly for Christians who have the hope of the resurrection through Jesus Christ, evasion and subterfuge about death are unnecessary.

This chapter will suggest ways to deal with the subject of death and answer those questions about heaven and hell that often come up at the time of death.

Obviously, children will react differently to the death of a family member than to that of a stray animal. Their reactions will be affected by many factors, such as age, emotional attachment to the dead person or animal, and the circumstances of death. Regardless of these factors, what is important is that as parents we offer plenty of support and encouragement to discuss feelings. For children to be comforted and not feel frightened or isolated, they must be given the opportunity to talk about what has happened.

Death of animals

Usually a youngster's earliest encounter with death is characterized more by curiosity than grief. Seeing a dead bird lying on the sidewalk as you walk with your four-year-old, for example, can give you a chance to help your child begin to form some concepts about death. Probably the child will want you to "fix" the "broken bird." You can explain that neither you nor anyone else can fix the bird, that it won't ever fly or eat or sing again. It is dead.

If the dead animal is a family pet, the child may appear heartbroken. I can remember now the intense, shaking grief I felt as a six-year-old on learning that my cocker spaniel was dead. From my vantage point of middle age, it seems one of the significant events of my childhood. One reaction of parents to the child's sorrow may be the suggestion that another pet be obtained immediately. For a time this idea often meets with resistance from the child. Many experts doubt the wisdom of this action. Let your child feel your sympathy as he or she grieves. This experience will strengthen the child for the future by preparing the youngster to face and overcome future losses. The replacement of a loved pet before grieving is completed may suggest to the child that everyone is replaceable, that love for pets and even people is so trivial it can be easily transferred from one to another.

Death of a child

Marguerite Rudolph in her book *Should the Children Know? Encounters with Death in Lives of Children* relates the following incident. Rachel, a four-year-old girl in the nursery school where Ms. Rudolph taught, died very suddenly. The teacher called together the other parents to discuss how they would tell the children about the death of their playmate and friend. The first parent to speak suggested the children be told Rachel had moved. Several parents agreed. Another suggested they say Rachel had taken a long trip and would not be back until after school was out. It took the teacher-author some time to convince many of the parents that talking honestly about Rachel's death was the best way to help her schoolmates deal with the tragedy.

If a playmate (or anyone else for that matter) has died, it's best not to say "God loved your friend so much that he took her to be with him in heaven." This remark can cause anxiety in the child who may fear that since God loves him too, he'll soon be ripped away from his mother and father and brought to live with a stranger named God.

This fear of separation underlies many questions young children ask about death. It isn't death so much that is feared as being taken away from parents. After all, if a playmate has been separated from parents in such a manner, the child may worry about meeting the same fate. It's comforting to tell your child that if people are reasonably careful about health and safety, almost always they will live to old age. Even though no one has a promise of longevity, a child under eight or nine needs frequent reassurance that he, other friends, or you as parents will not die for many years.

Death of a family member

The child who loses a parent or brother or sister confronts not only the overwhelming reality that the loved one is no longer alive, but even more, a feeling of isolation. Adults may react to the child's grief with cheerful, busy avoidance of sorrow or an embarrassed silence. This strenuous effort to avoid showing feelings can make grief much harder for the child.

If a death has occurred within the immediate family, the remaining members are likely to struggle along with shock, anger, depression, or guilt—leaving little emotional energy to support young children who remain. When there is no parent psychologically able to talk with the child, the child's feelings may "go underground." The youngster's grief may be hidden in a way that makes him or her appear apathetic or even callous. If the family member who has died is a sibling, the child's sorrow may be complicated by guilt—guilt that the child was not the one who died, yet relief to have been spared the accident or disease. In *Beat the Turtle Drum Slowly,* a beautifully written novel for young people, Constance Greene deals with the effect of a young girl's death on her younger sister.

> "Joss was their favorite," I said. "If I'd died instead of her, maybe they wouldn't feel so bad." It felt better just to say it out loud.
> "You know something," Mona folded the dishtowel and hung it up. "I bet Joss would've felt the same way. If it'd been you, she might've said the same thing. And both of you would've been wrong. I think when a child dies, it's the saddest thing that could ever happen. And the next saddest is the way brothers and sisters feel. They feel guilty because they fought or were jealous or a lot of things. And here they are alive, and the other one is dead. And there's nothing they can do. It'll take time, Kate."

Unless the child is unusual, the youngster may live in unspoken terror of losing his or her life in the same way. This fear may be recognized in marked behavior changes or excessive concern with health and safety. Obviously, such a situation needs attention, even if the child's fears have not been verbalized.

The child who loses a parent through death, however, loses much more than an important person. In Dr. Erna Furman's book, *A Child's Parent Dies*, she writes:

> When a parent dies, a child finds himself in a unique situation because of the very special nature of his ties to the deceased. An adult distributes his love among several meaningful relationships—his spouse, his parents, children, friends, colleagues—as well as in his work and hobbies. The child, by contrast, invests almost all his feelings in his parents. Except in very unusual circumstances, this single relationship is therefore incomparably rich and intense, unlike any close adult relationship. Only in childhood can death deprive an individual of so much opportunity to love and be loved and face him with so difficult a task of adaptation.

Jill Krementz' *How It Feels When a Parent Dies* relates 18 true stories of children who lost a parent, told in their own words. These moving accounts give us insight into what can be done at the time of a parent's death to help children through the trauma. Most of the children interviewed wished they had been allowed to attend both the funeral and burial and not be left out of something so important to them, as had happened to several of the children. Most authorities agree it is wise to include children in funerals. Children want and need to be with the rest of their families at such an important time, particularly if they have been prepared for what they will see and hear at the funeral or burial. Certainly this is the time when through our tears, we can share with children our faith that upholds us in the bleakest of times and our hope of eternal life.

Suggestions for explaining death to a child

1. Children under the age of six or seven have trouble comprehending death as final. Instead, it's often considered a reversible process, given the right conditions. "Dead" and "alive" are thought of more in terms of mobility than inherent life. Because of these and other misconceptions young children hold about death, it's good to determine what your child believes, then frame your answers to help develop reasonable concepts.

2. Listen to your child to learn hidden fears, then take them seriously—no matter how silly they seem to you. A child who has been told "Grandma just went to sleep" can understandably begin to panic at the thought of bedtime. Less obvious may be the avoidance of certain practices or places associated in the child's mind with the death. The child who may have wished angrily that mother or brother were dead may recall that hateful moment and be convinced of responsibility for the accident or illness that followed. One woman described such a guilty fear to me, saying that for years she carried such a burden, afraid her parents would find out that she, not a disease, was the real cause of her brother's death.

3. Prepare your children for the day they'll attend the funeral of someone close to them by taking them to the funeral of someone they don't know well. Many of children's questions relating to what happens to the body and the grisly folklore of children about the grave can be more easily answered without profound sorrow to complicate matters.

4. Be honest about your own grief. Your honesty gives permission for the child to cry, to talk about feelings, and to ask questions. At the same time, realize your child's reaction may seem inappropriate to you. After a violent storm of tears, the child may happily skip away to play. Children are not able to sustain any one mood or emotion—even grief— for the length of time adults do. It may appear shocking and hurtful to see

a child who appears to be so easily consoled, or worse yet, seems to need no comforting. Be patient and sensitive to the moment when the child is ready to talk. Nonverbal communication tells the child you're available for support and sympathy. Give lots of hugs at this time.

5. If a death occurs that deeply affects your child, be sure your child's teachers are aware of this. Otherwise, they may not be ready to help the child whose grief is showing up in the classroom as misbehavior.

Questions about death

If we take the kitten home and give it milk, will it come alive?
No. The kitten is dead. It can't eat or drink. Its body doesn't need food anymore.

Is the kitten all dead, or just the part where its leg is smashed?
The kitten is all dead. It can't move at all. It must have been injured worse than where you see its leg hurt.

Does the kitten need food when it's buried?
No. It will still be dead, just like now, and not need food.

Will the kitten be scared under the ground?
No. The kitten doesn't have any feelings now.

Will the kitten go to heaven?
We don't know for sure. The Bible says all creation will be changed and freed from decay. That sounds as though it might include kittens (Rom. 8:21).

Does grandma get cold when it snows on her grave?
I know you are worried about grandma, but she can't feel things like cold or pain anymore. She is happy and we can be happy for her, even though we miss her very much.

If grandma went to heaven like you said, why did we put her in the ground?

Grandma moved out of her body when she died. That's the part we put in the ground. Some day in the future, she'll receive a new and better body without the aches and pains of the old one.

Why are dead people buried?

There are many reasons. One of them is that soon after death, the body begins to smell bad. When it's buried, the body becomes part of the earth again. The Bible tells us God created people out of dust, and when we die, our bodies return to dust.

I heard about someone who was cremated. Is that wrong?

Sometimes people decide to have their bodies burned after death. That's all right too. No matter what is done to the body after death, when Jesus returns we'll all have new, resurrected bodies.

Why did grandma die?

(This question may mean, *Am I going to die and be separated from you too?* or *Are you going to die and leave me here by myself?* Reassure your child that usually people live to be old and by the time you die, your child will be grown and able to care for himself. Name people who would be around to care for him if he seems to need more assurance.)

(Or if your child is asking a specific question, you might say, "Ever since people chose to follow their own way instead of being like God, death has been a part of the world. Everything we know except God dies sometime. Grandma just reached the end of her life. Her body was old and worn out. But a better life is ahead for us, one with no sickness or death or sadness.")

Why doesn't heaven fall on us? There must be millions of people up there!

We often talk about heaven as though it's "up." Really, though, the kingdom of heaven isn't up or down or anyplace on a map. It's more like a time. So the number of people doesn't matter. There can't be too many in the kingdom of heaven.

How long does it take to get to heaven?

Time probably isn't measured after death like it is now. But Jesus told the dying robber on the cross, "Today you will be with me in paradise" (Luke 23:43). So it must seem to happen very quickly.

Can people who don't believe in God go to heaven?

This is a hard question. Some people say yes; some say no. We do know that God is able to do anything, because he's God. So we should be careful about saying what he can't or won't do. To be sure of heaven, though, all we need do is believe God has forgiven our sins because of what Jesus did for us. It's that simple.

Do I have to be religious to go to heaven?

It depends what you mean by religious. Jesus said the way to the kingdom is not to be religious but to trust him (John 6:28-30). Of course that doesn't mean we won't try to please God and be loving to people.

Won't heaven be boring? What will we do?

Heaven can't be boring or it wouldn't be heaven. For sure, we won't sit around playing harps and polishing halos. We will be perfectly happy and learn to be the people God intended us to be. It will be like being the happiest you've ever been in your life multiplied by a thousand.

What will my body be like in heaven?

It will be your body, but better. We won't need to breathe or eat. We won't ever be sick or hurt. Think of a butterfly emerging from a cocoon. It's the same creature yet more beautiful and in a form the worm going into the cocoon couldn't imagine. That's the best picture people have thought of to compare what our bodies will be like after death compared to now.

How will I get to heaven?

It won't be like any way you've traveled before. Since heaven isn't a place but a way of being, you won't need a plane or bicycle to get there.

Do people in heaven see us now?

Probably. The Bible says we are surrounded by "a great cloud of witnesses." The writer was speaking of people who have died.

Can I take my favorite things to heaven?

You may have carried around a blanket as a small child, but when you grew to be an older child, you didn't want it around anymore. It'll be like that in heaven. We will have outgrown things that seem so important to us now.

What will we wear in heaven?

The Bible describes the clothing we'll wear as "white garments." Since white is the color of light, that might mean we wear a type of clothing unlike anything we can imagine now, one that's made of light, reflected from the glory of God.

Will we know each other in heaven?

The best answer to this question is found in the New Testament. After Jesus had risen from the dead, his disciples recognized him, but not right away. He was the same Jesus they had known, yet he was different. They recognized him by the way he acted and what he did more than how he looked. It may be like that in heaven.

If I'm really good, will grandma come back? She told me once I'd be the death of her.

Grandma didn't mean you'd cause her death. She died from the effects of old age. Your being good won't change that.

What is hell? Is it hot?

Hell is being separated from God, the most terrible thing in the world we could possibly imagine. The Bible describes it as "hot" as a way of telling us how awful it is to be separated from God.

Will I go to hell?

Jesus promised eternal life with him for those who believe in him. That's another word for heaven. You never need to worry about hell when you have that promise of Jesus.

9

CAN MY BRAIN GET TOO FULL?

Questions about God's Creation

One of the things that sets children apart from most adults is their insatiable curiosity about the natural world God created. The Hebrews who wrote the Old Testament expressed that same wonder and amazement about God's creation, but usually we as busy, 20th-century parents have developed a blind eye to the marvelous world around us. We've forgotten the feeling of "Wow! This world is really some place to be!" If we try to be open to our children's questions about that world, we can find our own senses immeasurably sharpened. The first barefoot walk of spring on the tickling grass, the vision of a vast starry summer sky—these are real-and-now experiences that are too infrequent for adults who permit mundane activities to dictate days. That's why it's important that we watch for occasions to see God in nature with our children. The opportunities are everywhere to teach the majesty, the dependability, the creativity of God.

Annie Dillard, author of *Pilgrim at Tinker Creek*, is an example of a contemporary adult who looks at the natural world with the intensity and directness of a child. "If creation had been left up to me, I'm sure I wouldn't have had the imagination or courage to do more than shape a single, reasonably sized atom, smooth as a snowball, and let it go at that. No claims of any and all revelation could be so farfetched as a single giraffe.''

After observing natural surroundings and the wonder of our own selves, the next step for us is to teach that our appreciation for creation is best expressed by a sense of gratitude and responsibility for care of our world and ourselves. At a very young age children can begin to understand that we are caretakers of the creation and that we have an obligation to conserve and improve the world around us.

Children can learn about the dependability of God through observing the cycle of day and night, winter and summer. They can learn of the lavish diversity of creation and the magnificence of the universe through observing with parents such events as a meteor shower or a visit to a zoo or museum. We can lead children to encounter the world, showing proper and useful attitudes. We also need to know when to be silent, to let them experience God's handiwork without chatter that merely detracts from sights and scenes that need no words.

Over and above our amazement at far-flung galaxies, magnificent mountain vistas, intricacies of snowflakes and spider webs, we can help our children experience the awesomeness and miracle of life itself.

The Bible tells us that the crowning gem of God's creation is not Mount Everest or the Grand Canyon or even the Milky Way. It is you and I, men and women. The human mind that thinks, the emotions that flood us with feelings, the spirit that worships and yearns after God—these deserve admiration and thanksgiving from parents and children to the Creator of all goodness.

Questions about creation

How many stars are there?

No one knows, but in our own Milky Way galaxy, there are billions, and no one knows how many other galaxies exist. We cannot imagine how vast is God's creation. That makes God's love for each of us even more amazing.

Why do stars twinkle?

Stars don't twinkle, but they seem to because we look at them through an ocean of air. Even on clear nights bits of dust or clouds pass between us and the stars. That makes the starlight dim, then brighten.

Are there people on other planets?

Some scientists think the chances are good that some form of life exists on other planets. One reason is the materials of which we are made can be found in other parts of space. Another is that many stars in the universe seem to be like our sun. If someday we discover life on other planets, we will realize even more how powerful our Creator God is.

Why does the wind blow?

The wind blows because sunshine warms the earth. Then the earth warms the air that's close to it. When the air gets warm, it goes up, because it's lighter, and the cooler heavy air above it moves down to take its place. We feel that motion as wind. Another type of wind is caused by the motion of the earth itself as it rotates.

What makes the sun shine?

(For a young child, explain that God planned for the sun to keep us warm, give us light, and help crops to grow. Explain to older children that the sun keeps shining brightly year after year because it's burning hydrogen which frees energy over an extremely long period of time, unlike fuels such as coal or oil that are quickly consumed.)

Why is the sky blue?

The sky looks blue to us because sunlight is broken up by particles of dust and water in the atmosphere. That sunlight is made up of all colors of light, like a rainbow, but the blue part of the light is just the right wave-length to be scattered by those particles. So on a noncloudy day, the sky looks blue. But at dawn or sundown, the light of the sun passes through a thicker atmosphere than during the day, and red and orange colored waves are scattered.

(This is the type of explanation that's completely inappropriate for a three-year-old. Don't bother with technical explanations! Just say that God created the sky to be blue because God loves pretty things and wants us to be happy. We usually feel happy when the sky is blue.)

Can the sky fall down on me?
The sky isn't like a blanket that hangs over the world. It's open space that goes on farther than telescopes can see or spaceships can reach.

Where do clouds go when the sky is blue?
The sky always contains water. Sometimes it's like a gas, and we don't see it, as when the sky is cloudless. But if the temperature and other conditions are right, the water changes from gas to droplets of water, and we see that as clouds.

Why do leaves change color in the fall?
The leaves are green during the spring and summer because of green matter or chlorophyll that's needed to make food for the tree. Because the tree rests during the winter, it doesn't make chlorophyll any longer, and the leaves' other colors show up as they begin to decay, turning beautiful colors in the process.

What makes an echo?
The sound that is being echoed is reflected from an object such as a wall or mountain.

Why do birds sing?

Birds call to other birds to communicate. We think of these calls as singing. Birds may be calling to give a warning, to announce food, to attract a mate, and maybe for other reasons.

How many animals are there?

When we try to count kinds of animals, we get some idea of how much God must have enjoyed variety in his creation. It's impossible to count all the kinds of land, sea, and air animals that exist. Many are too small to be seen with the naked eye. Scientists have tried counting the number of species. Two animals are of the same species when they can mate and have babies that themselves can have babies. Lions, tigers, and housecats are all members of the cat family, but belong to different species. So far, around a million species have been discovered, most of them insects.

Why does a cat's fur stand up when it's afraid or angry?

Since cats can't tell people, we can only guess that they do this to frighten off some enemies. With other, biting enemies, the fur standing up may cause teeth to bite into fur instead of muscle and save the cat's life.

What animal is the fastest?

Cheetahs have been clocked at 70 miles an hour during a dash of 100 yards. They're probably the fastest animal.

What's the biggest number?

Mathematicians, or scientists who study numbers, believe that no matter how big a number we think of, there is one always bigger. That idea is called infinity and it has a special symbol: ∞ The largest number we give a name to is called a "googolplex." It is a 1 with a "googol" of zeros after it. A "googol" is a 1 with 100 zeros after it.

Why do dogs go round and round before they lie down?

Thousands of years ago, dogs would circle around, making a comfortable spot in the grass to lie down. Now, even though your dog has a soft rug to lie on, the habit has continued.

Why do cats purr?

No one seems to know just why. They purr when they're contented and comfortable. Purring seems to be a cat's way of smiling.

Why does water put out fire?

Water doesn't put out all kinds of fire, oil fires for example. But with most fires, water smothers the fire by preventing oxygen from getting to it. And fire can't burn without oxygen. It also cools the burning material below the temperature needed to burn.

Why did God make people?

Since no one can know the mind of God, we can only guess, based on what we do know about God. We know God created the world and everything in it. We can guess God wanted something more like himself than the rivers or valleys to love, so he created people. God created people "in his image," meaning we too are able to create and love.

How did people learn to talk?

God gave humans a special ability to communicate. Our speech probably began with sounds that described or imitated something. That's why young children learning to talk might call a dog a "bow-wow." As new words were needed, they were gradually added. Different words were added in different parts of the world. That's why there are languages we don't understand.

Can my brain ever get too full?

Unless your brain is diseased, it can go on almost forever learning and remembering things. The more you exercise your memory, the better it gets.

What makes me sneeze?

Your nose and other breathing passages are lined with a delicate type of skin or mucous membrane. When a tiny speck of dust or something else that doesn't belong there gets on this mucous membrane, we sneeze to get rid of that irritation.

Why do people have to sleep?

God gave not only people but animals the gift of sleep. When we sleep, everything that makes our bodies run smoothly while we're awake slows down. That gives the body a chance to cleanse itself of the waste products that build up in the brain and muscles when we're awake and the body is working hard.

What happens when I sleep?

The part of you that thinks and plans takes a rest. Your eyes close so you don't notice things you could see, and other than very loud noises, you don't hear what's going on. Your lungs and heart and other organs go on working but more slowly. Parts of your body that have worn out are replaced with new cells.

Why does an onion make me cry?

Onions give off a substance that makes tear glands produce tears quickly. These tears help protect the eye from the strong substance given off by the onion.

Why did I see stars when I bumped my head?

The nerves for seeing may get excited by a bump on the head. Whenever these nerves are excited in any way, we get the feeling of seeing light. Sometimes that light seems to show up like stars.

Why does my stomach hurt when I'm hungry?

It's another way God built in to protect people. We can't get so busy doing things we forget to eat when our stomach is hurting! When your stomach is empty, the brain signals it to expand and contract. It gives us a feeling of emptiness and wanting to find some food.

Why do people yawn?

Most of the time when you yawn, you're tired. Too much waste air and other materials are collecting in your muscles. When this happens, your brain signals your body it needs more oxygen, and without even thinking about it, you open your mouth, take in a huge breath of air and push out a lot of bad air. Sometimes you yawn because you see someone else yawn. The sight of a yawn can start your yawn muscles to working automatically.

Why do people hiccup?

The loud, sudden sound we call a hiccup is caused by two sets of muscles working against each other. The flap that closes your windpipe when you eat so no food goes down the wrong tube goes shut with a smack. At the same time, a big muscle— the diaphragm—that helps you breathe jerks up with a snap.

How many hairs do I have on my head?

Unless you're losing your hair, you have over 100,000 hairs on your head. And God tells us he understands and cares about us so much he knows how many hairs we have!

Why does hair turn grey?

Some hair cells contain coloring matter called pigment. It makes our hair look brown or red, for example. As our bodies age, these cells are no longer produced so the hair turns gray, then white, since there are no cells to color it.

Why are tears salty?

Pure water like you drink would hurt the delicate parts of your eye. The body's water needs to be slightly salty.

Why do I get goose bumps when I'm cold?

If you suddenly get frightened or chilled, a chemical is released in your body that makes muscles tighten up. You notice these tightened muscles most under your skin. They make your body hair stand straight up.

If I wasn't me, who would I be?

God created you and made you special. No one can ever take your place in the whole world. And you couldn't ever be anyone but the special person God created you to be. Psalm 139 says God knit you together or formed you inside your mother and knew what you'd be like before you were born. You can only be the special person God wants you to be.

10

WHY DOES RICKY LOOK DIFFERENT?

Questions about Disabilities, Prejudice, and Differences

Janie came home from school with a rather strange look on her face. "Mom, there's a new boy in my class. He looks so different. His face is like this," she grimaced, "and his head shakes, and he flaps his hands like a bird. Mom, why does Ricky look like that?"

Since the mid-1970s "mainstreaming" (putting children with serious disabilities back into regular classrooms) has made these children more visible. Children who in the past were usually hidden at home or in institutions now often can lead more normal lives. Probably your child will have a classmate who is severely hearing impaired and uses some sign language, or perhaps one who is wheelchair-restricted or blind. These visible disabling conditions are bound to raise questions and concerns. How do you deal with them?

And what about the child of another race who may be part of your child's life? Or the one who's considered "weird" by classmates—the effeminate little boy, or the girl who blinks nervously and whose behavior is immature, the one taunted as "baby." What do you teach your child about these differences?

How do you teach your child about being different from other children, about how to distinguish between positive and negative differences? How are you doing to teach which differences in others should be affirmed, and which, if any, should be influenced toward change? This chapter will offer some suggestions.

Our culture is frequently harsh in its treatment of people who appear different from what is supposedly "normal." For example, Greg came from a family where unrestrained enthusiasm for all sports was the rule. However, he much preferred to spend time reading or working quietly and meticulously on his insect collection. He was ridiculed by others in his family. "Queer," "Pansy" and "Buglover" were some of the labels applied to him. He grew more and more withdrawn, his self-esteem sinking into nonexistence. His uniqueness was totally unappreciated.

Music has always been extremely important to me. Some of my most enjoyable times have come from listening to or making music, so I was quite disappointed when Erik, my older son, decided early in life he didn't want piano lessons. In junior high, a brief fling with the violin failed to deepen into a long-term relationship, despite my proddings and suggestions. It's been hard for me to let Erik develop his own interests when they didn't (to date, at least) include one dear to my own heart. I'm sure many other parents have tried to similarly encourage or discourage qualities or interests in their children. When parents do this, it's easy for the child to begin feeling, "What I'm really like, what I like to do, isn't important. I must not be important."

Dr. Alvin H. Price and Jay A. Parry, authors of *101 Ways to Boost Your Child's Self-Esteem,* believe that to build children's self-esteem, parents need to allow for differences, for example, in how children approach life and what they like to do with themselves. This can be done by considering both differences between siblings and between children and parents, then planning activities that will attempt to satisfy everyone's needs and interests.

Disabling conditions

But what if those differences include disabling conditions that profoundly affect the child's activities and those of the family? People who work with such children seem to agree that to a large extent, the degree or kind of disability doesn't affect a child's life and happiness nearly as much as does the way the child feels about himself or herself and the disability. The important task for parents of a disabled child is to help the child face life with the disability in a way that maximizes strengths and realistically faces limitations. Even if you don't live with a disabling condition in the family, it's good to encourage those attitudes in children. Inform your child about disabilities. Research shows that children who are so informed and who have personal contact with disabled people have a more positive attitude than other children.

Young children are often frightened of a person with visible disabling conditions. People who exhibit uncontrolled muscular movements or wear leg braces, for example, may be threatening to youngsters who unconsciously fear something similar might happen to them. Since they don't understand what they see, children often act cruelly or strangely. Don't give the children the impression that handicaps are too terrible to talk about. Encourage their questions, then answer them matter-of-factly, not with pity or disgust.

Children who have a disabled sibling may feel the same fear as other children but also experience anger, loneliness, and guilt. Very young children may worry about "catching" the disability from a brother or sister in much the same way they may have caught chicken pox. Older children may worry about the future, wondering what will become of the child, if parental responsibility will eventually rest on their own shoulders. They are often filled with angry questions directed toward parents, or toward the disabled brother or sister who has disrupted their lives, or perhaps toward God. Sometimes they envy the time, attention, and money that seems to be lavished on the "special sibling."

After experiencing anger and envy (especially if these feelings have been verbalized or acted out toward the brother or sister), a person may also experience guilt. Children may also feel guilty because of the embarrassment they suffer when others stare at a handicapped brother or sister who drools or still plays with toddler toys. One woman, now a professor of special education, recalls the strange looks her disabled brother received, certain that everyone was wondering "what was wrong with the rest of us."

We parents can realize that difference disturbs adults as well as children and that we inadvertently convey our own anxiety to children. We want to protect our children from sadness or ridicule, but may have trouble conveying the proper attitude toward the disability of a friend's child or perhaps even our own. Do we treat it as a tragedy, a stigma, or merely a difference? As Helen Featherstone points out in *A Difference in the Family: Living with a Disabled Child*, "A child's disability challenges our values and the more severe the disability, the more forceful the challenge. What makes a life worth living? Is one life more important than another? Why do we value people?"

Whether your child has a disabled brother or sister or merely observes a person with a visible disabling condition, you should not deny the child's feelings. No one has been rid of anger or resentment simply because of a lecture on the *badness* of those feelings. Instead, parents can acknowledge them and go on to help the child identify with and begin to empathize with others. An autobiographical account of the effects on a family with a handicap begins: "All the members of my family are disabled. But most people recognize only the disability of my deaf sister." What is referred to in that statement is a fact that everyone needs to learn: handicapped people may be less handicapped than we think they are; likewise, "nonhandicapped" people, convinced of their superiority and self-sufficiency, can often be more handicapped than we realize.

Edward Sheldon, a New York playwright, seemed destined to become famous for his literary achievements when, in the early 1900s at the age of 30, he was cut down by a progressive arthritis so devastating that blindness followed total paralysis. Many people would have given up before reaching this level of disability. But Sheldon knew he had more to offer, that he was not the sum of his disability. He invited dozens of people to his bedside and encouraged and rejoiced with them. One was Anne Morrow Lindbergh who wrote, "One went away refreshed and stimulated, a hundred new paths shooting off in the mind. . . . The world opened up from those four closed walls." As parents, we can share with our chidlren what disabled people are capable of doing, instead of what they cannot do.

Racial differences

In contrast to their reaction to obvious physical disability, young children are generally conscious of racial differences without the taint of prejudice. As early as the age of three or four, awareness of racial differences appears, regardless of whether or not the child has been raised in an integrated environment.

While our son Erik was three, we had a teenage foster daughter of mixed race living with us. The first time her boyfriend, a jovial young black man, came to our home, he took Erik on his lap. Erik looked at him more and more searchingly from this close proximity before blurting out in honest amazement,

"Joe, did you know you're—*brown*?" We all laughed, even Joe, because it was obvious there was no value judgment in Erik's question. He hadn't yet learned some of the ugly messages the world teaches about racial differences.

On the other hand, our children are not very old before racial slurs or stereotypes impinge on them, from television advertising or programs, store decorations, or jokes from other children. In their book, *Parenting for Peace and Justice*, Kathleen and James McGinnis recount this story: "Theresa was only a year old and Tommy was about five. I was talking to Tommy about Theresa's Native American heritage, about what it means to be a member of the Winnebago Nation. He listened patiently to my explanation. Then he looked up and asked, 'Mommy, when Theresa grows up, will she kill us?' " The parents were shocked by the fear and misconceptions about people of other races that had been able to creep into their home. They understood in a flash how difficult the job of parents can be in teaching the value of all people, regardless of race or color.

As Christian parents we have a responsibility to teach our children that the body of Christ, the church, is made up of many nationalities and races. Just as all parts are important to the body's functioning, so are different cultures to be celebrated, not merely tolerated. On a planet where Christianity is growing faster in nonwhite cultures than in the Western world, parents need to help their children grow up learning that we are all builders in Christ's kingdom.

Individual differences

Related to the problems people can have in appreciating cultural differences are the questions children can have about individual differences. Most parents can think of times when their child has teased or been teased for being too fat, too thin, too dumb, too smart, too tall, too short, or a myriad of other reasons. Children whose behavior as well as appearance may be somewhat unusual may be targeted by others for cruelty and derision. How can we help children understand and appreciate their own uniqueness and that of others?

We had a child placed in our home who was diagnosed as suffering from "deprivational dwarfism." Although nearly ten, this boy weighed less than five-year-old John, and stood several inches shorter. He looked to be about four and had been teased for years about his size (apparently due to years of parental neglect). The child protection worker who had removed the boy from his home told us rather understatedly that his behavior could be "strange." After a day that included both obnoxious and dangerous acts, I began wondering what motivated this human cataclysm to behave in such unusual ways. What should we accept and what should we try to change?

Within the first day with us, he had pushed the screen from a second-story window and coaxed John out onto the roof with him before proceeding to pitch a phonograph, toys, and clothing to the ground below, all the while giggling gleefully. His appetite could best be described as voracious, and he hoarded food in unlikely places but nevertheless got up several times each night to forage in the refrigerator. A silly remark by a family member at dinner would set him off into uncontrollable, prolonged laughter, while he ran wildly around the table spitting food. To my despair, he would urinate anywhere, anytime the notion struck him. Gutteral, animal-like sounds were his favorite noises as he drifted off to a restless sleep. What images could Billy be carrying around about himself, I kept wondering, that created such unique and impossible behavior?

Billy seemed to take delight in the loud, the bizarre. It came as no surprise that he'd kept his elementary school in a constant state of uproar by disturbing actions and disruptive statements. Special teachers and psychologists tried heroically to help him with his behavior problems. Nothing seemed to help.

We noticed that while Billy was often severely depressed, moaning softly to himself as he ate or dressed, he also craved attention and constantly pointed out how bad he was. Within a few days, he claimed personal responsibility for (1) his mother's "nervous break-apart," as he called it, (2) his grandmother's heart attack, (3) his father's alcoholism, (4) parental abuse, and (5) other family problems. He truly seemed to believe he was the "baddest kid in the country" and found his identity and mission in life in those terms.

A child such as Billy who has a high sense of uniqueness is usually a problem for parents, family, teachers, and playmates. Such a child is not adaptive to doing what the group does or even getting along with the group. People believe such a child is trying to be different when actually he is being himself. Billy was called "weird" (and worse) by his classmates and teachers, because he was more inclined to follow his own feelings than the expectations of others. In a subsequent psychiatric evaluation, his extremely negative self-concept was described. Billy persisted in acting in a way he knew would bring pain and punishment. Why? He saw no choice but to live up to his negative sense of self, and, like most children, had found negative attention better than no attention.

During Billy's evaluation in our home, he expressed real problems with honest praise. Being told he had done a good job of cleaning up the bedroom made him nervous and uncomfortable. He couldn't fit praise into his self-concept as "the baddest kid."

Making Billy learn to feel good about himself after 10 years of parental abuse and neglect meant changing his self-concept, a task of which we weren't capable. He's now at a treatment center in another state, where he's expected to live for several years. Although Billy is an extreme example of how a child can be different, it's likely that occasionally your child is concerned too with personal or other children's differences. The following are general guidelines to help children feel good about their uniqueness and that of other children.

1. Accept the child even when you don't accept the behavior. This isn't an easy thing to do! Help the child to know it's OK to have unique likes and dislikes and opinions. Children don't suffer from being different; they ache from believing the differences are unacceptable.

2. Never ridicule or negatively label. Carelessly or angrily tossed-out labels sometimes haunt children into their maturity and old age. Pain and embarrassment from labels are often effective in the short run for inhibiting undesirable behavior, but at far too great a cost! When criticism is necessary, direct it to what needs improvement, not the child. Negative labels such as *brat, crybaby, liar, whiner, stupid,* destroy self-esteem. They most often are believed, and unconsciously the child attempts to live up (or down) to the label, just as Billy attempted to fulfill his self-concept of "the baddest kid."

3. Recognize your child's special traits or qualities: "You have a way of knowing when I'm sad and cheering me up!" "With those nice long legs you might be a really fast runner some day."

4. Encourage humor. If your child has a physical quality for which he or she is sometimes teased, encourage your child to use humor to fend off cruel statements from other children. For all but the most persistent taunters, humor will be disarming.

5. Treat each child as an individual. In an effort to be fair to children, many parents try to treat them equally and collectively. It's much easier to deal with children as a unit rather than to take the time and effort to acknowledge individual tastes, opinions, and differences. If parents convey respect for each child's differences, most likely the child will feel good about them too.

Children's questions about disabilities

Can I get the same sickness as Linda [a chronic one such as muscular dystrophy]?

Linda's illness is very rare and not a "catching" one.

Why isn't Jackie smart like me?

Not everyone can do things equally well. We can try to do our best and be patient with those who don't do some things as well as we do. Jackie might need extra help with some activities, but there is still plenty she can do.

What does "retard" mean? Someone called Jackie a "retard."

That's a cruel slang term for someone who has problems in learning. Jackie is much more than a retarded person, and that word limits her.

How did Jackie get like that?

Sometimes people who have a hard time learning had a birth injury. Other times something happened before birth. An older person could have an injury or disease that could cause the same problem.

Why does Jackie drool?

The muscles that tell her when to swallow aren't well developed. You don't drool, because your muscles and nerves tell you when you need to swallow, without your even thinking about it.

Why does Tom talk so loud? Why does his voice sound funny?

Tom is hearing-impaired, so he can't hear how loud his voice sounds to us. And because we learn to talk by listening to other voices, he has trouble knowing exactly how loud his voice should sound.

Why was Mary born blind? Was it your fault [or God's fault]?

No one knows for sure. For a while I thought maybe it was my fault, but the doctor told me it wasn't. It wasn't God's fault either. Some people might say it was God's will that Mary be blind, but God never wants bad things to happen to anyone.

Once I wished something terrible would happen to Annie, and right after that she found out she had cancer. Was that my fault?

(This question is one often left unspoken but is powerfully present in the child's mind.) Wishes like that aren't magic. You don't wish illness on people. Everyone gets sick at times, but not because someone wished them to be sick.

Sometimes I hate Sandy because he looks so weird. Is that wrong?

We all have problems at times with our feelings about people who are different. Can you think of some of the things you like about Sandy, or things you have in common?

Is Johnny ever going to be all right?

Johnny's spinal-cord is injured [or whatever the permanent disability might be] and no matter what, he isn't going to be able to walk or run again. But there are many things he can do. Let's concentrate on those.

What does it feel like to be in a wheelchair [blind, etc.]?

(Suggest a visit to a hospital supply store. Ask the manager if the child might examine wheelchairs, braces, and prostheses, and have their uses explained. Point out how stairs and narrow doorways often exclude many people from getting into buildings. Experiment with blindfolding your child for a short time while you watch to prevent anything dangerous from happening. Talk about a time your child had an accident or injury. Did the knee gash change the way he or she felt about everything else in her life? Of course not. Help your child to realize how people look or act because of a disability isn't the only important thing about them.)

How do deaf people learn to talk?

Deaf people learn to speak with special teachers who help them use their voices. Most deaf people's voices work with special help. Some use sign language and lip reading too.

Why do you spend so much time with Tim [a disabled sibling]?

He has special needs because of his condition. I'll spend extra time with you when you have special needs too. Remember when you needed help with your multiplication tables? I'll try to be there whenever you need me.

Questions about racial differences

My teacher said many people are prejudiced. What is prejudice, anyway?

The way we usually use the word means a person is judged before we know him because of his color or his race or religion or some other group of which he's a part. Usually it means a dislike or hatred of the people in that group.

Do white people ever turn black?

God created different races, and they have different shades of skin, just as flowers come in many colors. Black people can't turn white or white people turn black any more than a yellow flower can turn red.

Does God love some races more than others?

The color of a person's skin doesn't matter to God as much as what's in their hearts. There are good and bad people of all races.

A boy at school has a sticker on his bike that says, "Black is beautiful." What does that mean?

For a long time, black people in America were taught that their blackness was bad. "Black is beautiful" is a slogan that helped black people have pride in themselves. We could say that about all the colors that people come in.

Questions about differences

Why does Becky act like such a show-off, running around the room and yelling?

Becky may feel bad about herself and be asking for people to pay attention to her. Or she may have a physical problem that makes it hard for her to sit still. Whatever the cause, it's a good idea to be her friend however you can.

Ronnie always says he likes things everyone else in the class doesn't. Why does he do that?

It's OK to have opinions that are different from other people. You're the only one in our family who likes liver, remember? Everyone is entitled to his or her opinion.

Mike is so fat. The kids at school call him "Blubber." Why does he eat so much?

Sometimes people are heavy for reasons other than eating too much. He may have a medical problem. For whatever reason, he doesn't need another problem of kids making fun of him. Remember, God made people in all shapes and sizes, and he loves them all.

Marcia sucks her thumb when she doesn't think anyone is looking. Why doesn't she stop being such a baby?

Maybe Marcia feels lonely or afraid. Can you think of something you could do to make her feel happy?

Tom is a bully and beats up on kids who are smaller. Are you going to say that's OK too?

No, that behavior hurts people. Try to remember, though, about liking the person even if we don't like what he's doing. Look for times you can show kindness or friendliness to Tom, and you'll see him being less of a bully. Love changes people.

11

WHERE DO YOU GO ALL DAY, DADDY?

Questions about Work and Money

Although from infancy children notice one or possibly both parents leaving the home daily for several hours, most are probably only vaguely aware of what those parents do for a living. Many misconceptions exist in children's minds about employment and money, and recently unemployment is a reality with which many parents have had to deal, one that has raised its own questions in children's minds.

Probably every adult remembers being asked countless times, "What will you be when you grow up?" As a child, it took me a long time to make the connection between that question and choice of occupation. When we think about what is being asked ("What will you *be*?") and what is meant ("What is your intended occupation?"), we catch a sense of the enormous importance of work in our lives. It defines our very being to people who know nothing about us but our occupation. And yet, whether it be in a paid capacity or unpaid, the world of work remains confusing to most children. Few youngsters understand the connection, for example, between work and money.

Very young children have problems understanding white-collar work. Occupational prestige counts not at all with them.

When Erik was three, he aspired to be a garbage collector. From his point of view, the job of driving a truck along an alley and waving at people in their yards as the dumpster was guided into position was an appealing one. His own father's occupation as a pastor wasn't the least attractive. "You have to talk too long," he'd say. (Even the pastor's son didn't understand that Sunday morning preaching is only part of the occupation.)

Working conditions become important to children at six or seven when they realize how much of one's day is spent on the job. John, our younger son, has planned for some time to be a paleontologist who digs up dinosaurs. This child, who will go to extreme measures to keep his face out of water, was upset to learn many fossiles lie submerged in lakes and oceans. It was a discovery that only momentarily deterred him from his goal. "I'll leave those dinosaurs for the scuba divers," he decided.

Work as Christian vocation

Christian parents can help their children to see that while we can glorify and serve God in our occupations, we do so in a larger sense through our vocations. Often used synonymously today, *occupation* and *vocation* do not necessarily mean the same thing. *Vocation* is best understood in terms of a calling: we are called to love and serve and witness to God. Christian vocation answers the question, "Does my life have a purpose?" The answer is "Yes, in life with God shared with others."

Our vocation can be acted out through our occupations (which might change several times through our lifetimes). Our vocation remains constant. When parents explain what is involved in certain occupations, they can stress potential for service rather than how much money or prestige that occupation would afford. Too often children have been pushed toward career choices for only the most selfish of reasons.

Working mothers

While the older child usually has some idea of why one parent (generally the father) must leave home daily to "bring home the bacon," there may be less understanding of why the second parent leaves daily, especially if it is the mother, who until that time has always been around. If the mother herself has mixed feelings about why she's going to work or feels guilty about it, parents may have a tough time explaining this to children.

The truly liberated wife and mother of today knows she has many choices. She can choose to stay at home with her children, enjoying and nurturing their everyday growth and activities. Or because of economic or psychological needs, she can be employed part- or full-time out of the home. Whatever her choices, if the mother is personally satisfied, her children will probably do well. A mother who stays home all day bored and frustrated is no less destructive to her children than a mother who hates her job and comes home to her children irritable and overtired.

However, many mothers today are going off to work outside the home because of economic necessity, feeling divided about their choice. Increasingly, many couples find it impossible to pay for the standard of living they desire without two paychecks (and often, not even then). Before teaching children about money, it's helpful to seriously think about our own attitudes toward stewardship of financial resources.

Christian stewardship

Kathleen and James McGinnis' book, *Parenting for Peace and Justice,* deals beautifully and at length with the topic of Christian stewardship in the family. They point out that for Christians, "what is mine is not mine for my own exclusive use, but for the welfare of others."

"There are two elements of stewardship that are integral to its functioning in our lives. One is the source of what we have. The other is our own accountability," they write. Whatever we teach our children about money and possessions and employment should be set within that framework. All good gifts come from God, not from our own efforts, and we are responsible to God for how we use those gifts. For some reason, most Christian parents, myself included, who intellectually believe this, have problems translating ideas into life-style. Why is this so?

American Christians grow up in a society that relentlessly preaches conspicuous consumption. It tells us to go ahead and call ourselves Christian, but please, not to "get carried away," act or look any different from non-Christians in our life-styles. So we treat as unimportant Jesus' admonition to care for the poor, to live simply, to take up our cross. And when we give, scarcely ever do we give sacrificially, like the widow with her mite. Instead, for many people it's five or ten dollars dropped into the offering plate, or a dollar given to the neighbor collecting for March of Dimes. Children are watching. They see these transactions. And they see the outlays made for recreational vehicles or vacation trips or other luxuries, and they know without asking what is really important to parents.

We tell ourselves and our children that we've worked hard, that we deserve this new boat, diamond ring, this food processor, or asparagus steamer: "I work hard. I deserve it." Whenever I hear these words, I think of my friend who grew up in India, who tells of what life can be like there. She tells of men who supported large families by going to the docks before dawn, hoping they might be one of the few chosen to work that day, and if they were, these men would unload and carry burdens in 100° temperatures from dawn until dark. Even though the surface of the docks reached fiery temperatures, none of the men could afford shoes and instead wadded newspapers into pads and tied them around their feet. After 12 or more hours of manual labor in the most oppressive, humid working conditions imaginable, the men would be paid the equivalent of 50 cents. If they'd been fortunate enough to get work that day, they'd then be able to buy rice for the evening meal, rice that might feed the man, his family, and his elderly dependents.

Her statements take shape in my mind now whenever I hear someone say, "I work hard. I deserve it." I wonder what God thinks, the God who time after time sides with the poor, the weak, the oppressed. Until we start to take seriously the idea that what is ours is ours only in the sense that God is asking us to be managers, the poor will continue to starve, and the church will merely dream of the mission it could carry out.

If we believe in stewardship as an integral part of our faith, our giving will reflect that. We will thoughtfully and prayerfully arrive at a percentage of income to return to God. (Ten percent was the tithe of Jewish law.) After giving it, we'll manage on the other 90% or whatever might be left. And should our income rise, we'll joyfully increase the percentage we return for God's use. We'll encourage our children from a young age to put aside a portion of their gift money or allowance for the same purpose, explaining why as parents we give generously to the work of the Lord.

Money

Until the age of five or six, the average child has little conception of money as a medium of exchange. Barter, the exchange of goods or services, is much less abstract; therefore trade is understood long before the complexities of money.

As adults, we've probably forgotten how confusing it all seemed. Several difficult ideas are involved which we now take for granted. The most obvious is that ten cents is ten cents whether represented by a dime, two nickels, or ten pennies.

Most children under five or six would choose the ten pennies over a dime. The value to a young child lies in the number of items or perhaps some quality such as shininess. Only after reaching school age does the child understand that money's worth is not intrinsic, but in what it can buy.

The idea that only nations can make money is difficult too, especially when we use idiomatic expressions such as "He makes a lot of money." In these days of cash vending machines, it's easy to see why children can't conceptualize the process through which money is backed and printed, and how and why it circulates. As we move more and more into a cashless society, the intricacies will seem ever more baffling to young children. Credit, profit, and loss are as incomprehensible to children as the International Monetary Fund is to me. These are concepts that will be learned in the child's own time. More important than teaching the technicalities of money is teaching the value and dignity of work.

Teaching children about work

Most young children want to work, to help around the house and yard. Often, however, their attempts lead to such exasperation on the part of parents that they soon learn not to offer.

When they are willing to work alongside you, take the opportunity and praise whatever can honestly be commended, even if it's their willingness to help. Give them only as much as they're ready for and don't insist on perfection. Because a young child's willingness is fragile, it's more important to encourage that than to strive for the ultimate in performance.

Because for young children the expression "going to work" is meaningless, explain through objects or materials used in your work some aspect of your job. Even white-collar jobs use objects that lend themselves to this type of demonstration. My children, for example, are fascinated by the investigative brief-case I keep at home while on call for child-abuse complaints. An instant camera for taking trauma pictures, a tape recorder for statements, a pager, and various forms, along with an explanation of how they're used, helps them better understand what's involved in my work.

When a child leaves a job uncompleted, it's easy just to do the job yourself, but if the job is appropriate for the child's age, make the child finish it. To do the job yourself robs the child of self-esteem. Instead, remind the child that there's no TV or outside playtime until the task is done. The child who learns to finish age-appropriate jobs will grow in self-esteem and learn perseverance and responsibility needed in future years as a "professional" worker.

Questions about work

Do you have to work?

I work for many reasons. One of them is to earn money to buy things we need. Another is that work is good, and I enjoy it. Even people who have plenty of money and don't need to work usually like to because it's enjoyable.

Why do you want to work?

I like making [or doing] something for other people. I like being with other people and sharing their ideas.

What do you do all day?

(Explain in as specific ways as possible some of the tasks that make up your job.)

Why did you decide to be a teacher [or other vocation]?

(Mention factors that led you to your occupational choice, including how it fits into your Christian vocation.)

How do you become a teacher?

(As you answer this question, remember that small children have little or no understanding of processes occurring over a long period of time, such as education. They do understand repetitions and trying hard to do better next time, so attempt to frame your answer within those terms.)

Do you always have to be a teacher?

(Explain that many people change occupations through their lives because their lives change. Give examples of people you may know whose jobs have become obsolete and who were challenged to find new occupations, or people who felt God calling them to other occupations, perhaps ones in which they felt they could better serve God.)

What is the best job?

There's no "best job"! Depending on the gifts and abilities God has given you, you may find you're best suited to being a teacher or farmer or business person, or maybe something you've never even heard of yet.

Are some jobs better than others?

Any job that is honest and does not harm people or get money through cheating is a good job and worth doing well. Any job can be used to show our love of God and his people. Martin Luther said once a maid with a broom can show as much love for the people she works for as does the priest before the altar, who speaks of the love of Christ.

Questions about money

Why do we need to use money? Why won't the person at the store give us what we need?

The person running the store must pay for the food. The people who grew the food and brought it to the store also must be paid. Money is what we use to make sure everyone gets something for what they've done or made.

Why can't you just write a check if you're out of money?

A check is really a piece of paper that tells someone, "In the bank I have money to pay you for what I'm buying." If I don't have that money in the bank, I'm lying to that person.

How much money do we have to give to church?

We don't *have* to give any money to the church, but that wouldn't be right, any more than it would be not to help with expenses of schools that give you an education. We gain so much in our lives from the church that it's only fair to help with its expenses.

A man on TV said the more money I give to God, the more he'll give me back. If I give my whole allowance to church, will I get it back doubled?

Probably not. The reason we give to God shouldn't be from selfish motives. We give because God's given to us, and we want to share with others. We have God's promise to provide for us, and that's good enough.

Why do we have to share? Why can't God give people what they need so we don't have to give them food or money?

God has given plenty of food and everything else we need to all people. It's up to us to make sure everyone gets what they need by sharing, because we have far more than we need.

How do you decide how much money to give to the church?

Once a year, we sit down and figure out how much money we think we'll earn that year. Then we figure out a part of it, called a percentage, and give some of it weekly or monthly to our church. We're happy to give it since God has been so good to us.

Why don't we use gold coins like in the olden days?

Gold can get very heavy to carry around. People started using paper money instead, which is like the government's check, because it's more convenient.

Why does the clerk at the grocery store give you back money when you use dollars, but not when you write a check?

(The idea of making change is a difficult one until a child reaches the age of seven or eight. A child of seven might believe, for example, that if a clerk really likes you, he'll give you change. If he doesn't know you, he won't. Eventually the child learns that niceness or means of payment doesn't affect credit.)

Why can't people make their own money?

Money wouldn't be worth anything if everyone could make it. Only countries can make money. People who try to illegally print money are called counterfeiters and may go to prison.

Somebody said money is the root of all evil. Why do you work for money then?

The Bible says the *love* of money is a root of all kinds of evil (1 Tim. 6:10). Like almost anything else, money can be used for good or bad. When it's used well, it can feed people, make them well, and, in general, serve and glorify God.

Questions about unemployment

Why aren't you going to work anymore?

Because there wasn't enough work for all the people at my plant, I'm "laid off." That means for now, I'm not going to work. (Or) I'm hoping to find a job that will be more dependable. (If you use the word "fired" in your answer, be aware that many small children associate the word with burning or danger. Explain that it means your job was ended.)

How will we eat?

We won't go hungry. I'll get unemployment money for a while. If I haven't found a new job when that money runs out, we can borrow money. We will go without some things you're used to, but we'll be together, and we'll have enough to eat.

Did you get fired because you were bad?

(Explain as concretely as possible why your job was terminated, without getting into issues such as the national economy. Stress the fact that you'll begin looking right away for other work and that the family will be all right even if some sacrifices are required.)

12

WHEN YOU DON'T HAVE THE ANSWERS

"I wonder if I'll live to grow up or if the world will blow up before then."

"What can just one person do, anyway, to prevent the bomb from killing the earth?"

These statements and others chillingly similar were made by upper-elementary students when asked what they thought the future would bring. Behavioral scientists are no longer surprised to find that children often fear the likelihood of nuclear war in their lifetime. Often starting as young as five or six, these children are growing up afraid of "danger, death, sadness, corruption, explosion, cancer, bombs, pollution, terrible devaluing of human life." These associations were among those mentioned in a 1978 study by Harvard child psychiatrists John Mack and William Beardsley.

Similar findings have been reported by other social scientists. The evidence is mounting that American children increasingly suffer nightmares, vague depression, and a sense that they won't live long enough to grow up. The evidence also shows most parents feel unable or unwilling to deal with these feelings. Parents and children may try to mutually protect one another. Children may avoid bringing up their concerns over what they think the parents can't handle. Likewise, parents don't talk about their own concerns to protect their children from the pain of an issue that doesn't have a comfortable answer.

The possibility of nuclear holocaust is probably the foremost danger that confronts parents who see their responsibility as ushering children safely into their own adulthood. But there are other scary shadows lurking out there too, ones that make us lie awake, wondering, in the dead of night. How can we prepare our children for the not-far-off day when through genetic advances, human life can be remade?

Scientists describe the funseekers of the next decade hooking themselves to terminals that excite the pleasure centers of the brain. In the future people may spend most of their hours indulging their insatiable craving for pleasure by artificial stimulation of their brains.

We live today with confusing and confused values and philosophies rampant in society. Even people who seek to live a Christian life hear a babble of contradictory beliefs and viewpoints. The strident but popular voices of many religious figures of today remind us of Paul's warning to Timothy: "For the time will come when men will not put up with sound doctrine. Instead, to suit their own desires, they will gather around them a great number of teachers to say what their itching ears want to hear. They will turn their ears away from the truth and turn aside to myths" (2 Tim. 4:3-4).

Profound changes in the way children are conceived, carried, and born are already happening. Advances in the knowledge of the body's immune system and other technologies hint that human immortality through body transplants is a few years around the corner. Changes in the way people communicate with each other make thoughtful people uneasy. Promised computers that can read our minds, making today's computer language obsolete, raise the specter of Orwell's Big Brother.

Where in all these changes, real or potential, do we place the value of the human soul, of Christ's sacrifice, of faith and grace and service?

In the face of such wonderful and terrible changes, does the God of the Bible have a place? Can the ancient God who talked to simple nomads like Abraham and Moses seem relevant to future generations living in the marvels of technology? Yes. The most basic emotional needs for people will always be love, security, and acceptance. For persons living in Jesus' day or in the 21st century, these needs are the same. Christian parents have a unique ability to give their children the gift of meaning and hope for an uncertain future. For only in Christ does the world find its undeserved hope.

As I finish writing this chapter, one of the longest, coldest, most unpleasant winters I've experienced has ended. Around me, the spring that came at first hesitantly and with many false starts, now explodes with warmth and color and song. Neighbors again lean over their fences to visit, and lawn mowers growl pleasantly through the Saturday afternoon stillness. It's one more reminder to me of the eternal, unchanging reality of God.

Somehow, with this reassurance of God's promise of faithfulness, I remember that faithfulness is all God expects of us. My inadequacies and failings as a person and a parent are forgiven. I wish I could start over at the beginning and be a better parent from the moment of each child's conception. But that's not possible, so we go forward, doing what we can with God's grace.

I'll never have all the answers. I won't even know all the questions. But that's all right. The words of the old hymn form a prayer for myself and my children:

> Change and decay in all around I see
> O thou who changest not, abide with me.

That too is my prayer for you and your children.

BIBLIOGRAPHY

Briggs, Dorothy Corkille. *Your Child's Self-Esteem: The Key to Life.* Garden City, N.Y.: Doubleday and Company, 1975.

Buechner, Frederick. *The Magnificent Defeat.* New York: Seabury, 1961.

Buechner, Frederick. *Wishful Thinking: A Theological Age.* New York: Harper & Row, 1971.

Campbell, D. Ross, M.D. *How to Really Love Your Child.* Wheaton, Ill.: Victor Books, 1983.

Coopersmith, Stanley. *Antecedents of Self-Esteem.* San Francisco: W. H. Freeman and Company, 1967.

Dillard, Annie. *Pilgrim at Tinker Creek.* New York: Bantam, 1975.

Drescher, John M. *If I Were Starting My Family Again.* Nashville: Abingdon, 1971.

Furman, Erna. *A Child's Parent Dies.* New Haven: Yale University Press, 1974.

Greene, Constance. *Beat the Turtle Drum Slowly.* New York: Viking, 1976.

Krementz, Jill. *How It Feels When a Parent Dies.* New York: Knopf, 1981.

McGinnis, James and Kathleen. *Parenting for Peace and Justice.* Maryknoll, N.Y.: Orbis, 1983.

Nelson, Gerald. E., M.D. *The One Minute Scolding.* Boulder: Shambla Books, 1984.

Parry, Jay A. and Dr. Alvin A. Price. *101 Ways to Boost Your Child's Self-Esteem.* Wauwatosa, Wis.: American Baby Books, 1982.

Satir, Virginia, *Peoplemaking.* Palo Alto: Science and Behavior Books, 1972.

Seuss, Dr. *Horton Hears a Who.* New York: Random House, 1954.

Shedd, Charlie. *Promises to Peter.* Waco: Word, 1970.

Rudolph, Marguerite. *Should the Children Know? Encounters with Death in the Lives of Children.* New York: Schocken Books, 1978.

Westerhoff, John H. *Will Our Children Have Faith?* New York: Seabury, 1976.

White, William R. *Speaking in Stories.* Minneapolis: Augsburg, 1982.